3.22.78

EASY
ESSAYS

EASY ESSAYS

By Peter Maurin
with woodcuts by Fritz Eichenberg

FRANCISCAN HERALD PRESS
1434 West 51st Street • Chicago, Illinois 60609

Easy Essays by Peter Maurin was last published in 1961 by
Academy Guild Press. New edition copyright © 1977 by
Franciscan Herald Press, 1434 West 51st Street, Chicago, Illinois
60609. Reprinted with permission.

Library of Congress Cataloging in Publication Data

Maurin, Peter.
  Easy Essays (The green revolution).

  Reprint of the 2d rev. ed. published in 1961
by Academy Guild Press, Fresno, Calif.
  Published in 1949 under title: Catholic
radicalism.
  1. Church and social problems—Catholic
Church—Addresses, essays, lectures. I. Title.
HN37.C3M53 1977   261.8′3   77–24357
ISBN 0–8199–0681–6

When I first saw Peter Maurin* my impression was of a short, broad-shouldered workingman with a high, broad head covered with greying hair. His face was weatherbeaten, he had warm grey eyes and a wide, pleasant mouth. The collar of his shirt was dirty, but he had tried to dress up by wearing a tie and a suit which looked as though he had slept in it. (As I found out afterward, indeed he had.)

What struck me first about him was that he was one of those people who talked you deaf, dumb and blind, who each time he saw you began his conversation just where he had left off at the previous meeting, and never stopped unless you begged for rest, and that was not for long. He was irrepressible and he was incapable of taking offense.

The night I met Peter I had come from an assignment for *The Commonweal*, covering the Communist-inspired "hunger march" of the unemployed to Washington. I had prayed at the Shrine of the Immaculate Conception, on the Feast of the Immaculate Conception, that I might find something to do in the social order besides reporting conditions. I wanted to change them, not just report them, but I had lost faith in revolution. I wanted to love my enemy, whether capitalist or Communist.

I certainly did not realize at first that I had my answer in Peter Maurin. I was thirty-five years old and I had met plenty of radicals in my time and plenty of crackpots, too: people who had blueprints to change the social order were a dime a dozen around Union Square.

At that time Peter Maurin was fifty-seven, had never married, had been "away from the Church" in his youth, had worked with Sangnier and his social studies group in Paris, and had sold its paper, *Le Sillon*. He believed in going to the people in town and country-side, because first of all he was of the people himself.

---

*Much of this material appeared in *Jubilee*, March, 1960. (Copyright 1960 by the A.M.D.G. Publishing Co.) as "I Remember Peter Maurin." We gratefully acknowledge permission to use it.

He was born in a tiny hamlet in the southern part of France, 200 miles from Barcelona, one of a family of 24 children. His own mother had died after she had born her fifth child, and his stepmother had had 19 and was still alive, he said.

"I did not like the idea of revolution," he once told me. "I did not like the French revolution, nor the English revolution. I did not wish to work to perpetuate the proletariat. I never became a member of a union, even though here in America I did all kinds of hard labor. I was always interested in the land and man's life on the land. That is why I went homesteading in Canada, but after two years, after my partner was killed in a hunting accident, I went around Canada with work gangs and entered this country in 1911, where I have been ever since."

When I first knew Peter I was busy at a research job which kept me at the library until three in the afternoon. When I got home to my little apartment on East Fifteenth Street, I'd find him there waiting for me, ready to indoctrinate, to give me a lesson in history from the Catholic point of view. He had been sent to me, he said, by George Shuster, later president of Hunter College, who at that time was editor of *The Commonweal*. George thought that we were alike in point of view, both interested in changing the social order and in reaching the masses with the social teachings of the Church.

I had been a Catholic only about four years, and Peter, having suggested that I get out a paper to reach the man in the street, started right in on my education; he was a born teacher, and any park bench, coffee shop counter, bus or lodging house was a place to teach. He believed in starting on a program at once, without waiting to acquire classroom or office or meeting hall. To reach the man in the street, you went to the street. Peter was literal.

I had met Peter in December, 1932, and the first issue of *The Catholic Worker* came out in time for the May Day celebration in Union Square, 1933. What Peter Maurin was interested in was the publication of his essays, and my journalistic sense led me to report conditions as they were, to paint a picture of poverty and destitution, homelessness and unemployment, in short, to so arouse the conscience that the reader would be willing and ready to listen to Peter when he talked about things as they should be.

Peter was very much afraid of class war, and after his first essays were published he could not quite understand why I wrote so much about interracial injustice, hard conditions of labor, inadequate housing. He much preferred to write about how things should be—Houses of Hospitality for the needy, charity exercised in every home, voluntary poverty and the works of mercy, farming communes and agronomic universities that would teach people to earn a living by the sweat of their own brows instead of someone else's.

The Catholic Worker was financed like the publications of any radical "splinter group." If we had had a mimeograph machine, it would have been a mimeographed paper. But we had nothing but my typewriter, so we took our writing to a printer, found out it would cost $57 to get out 2,500 copies of a small, eight-page sheet the size of *The Nation,* and boldly had it set up. There were no office, no staff, no mailing list. I had a small pay-check coming in for the research job which was just finishing; two checks were due for articles I had written, but these were needed to pay overdue rent and light bills. Father Joseph McSorley, the Paulist, paid me generously for a small job of bibliography which I did for him; the late Father Ahearn, pastor of a Negro church in Newark, gave me ten dollars; Sister Peter Claver gave me one dollar which someone had just given her. Those were our finances. We took that first issue of the paper into Union Square that May Day and sold it for one penny a copy to Communists and trade-unionists.

Peter slept in the back of *The Catholic Worker* office, and he soon brought in an Armenian anarchist poet and a German agnostic to share his quarters with him and to provide sparring partners for round-table discussions. He never took part in any of the work of the paper, except to turn in each month half a dozen "easy essays," many of which he insisted that we repeat over and over again. He was the kind of teacher who believed in repetition, restatement, and the continual return to first principles. He loved, however, to see visitors, and, if none came into the office, he went out into the highways and byways and found them. He ranged the island of Manhattan from end to end, visiting brokers on Wall Street and Negroes on the street-corners in Harlem.

The only time Peter got excited was when he found others agreeing with him, approving his ideas. Then his voice would rise, his eyes would shine and he would shout out exultingly. He always expected so much in the way of results that I often felt called upon to put a damper on him, to tone down his optimistic enthusiasms. But I soon noticed that he was never depressed or discouraged by disappointments or failures.

A failure such as that of the first round-table discussion was an example. Peter had hoped for great results from a series of Sunday afternoon discussions he had planned. Optimistically, for the first one he rented the ballroom of the Manhattan Lyceum, where trade union conventions as well as balls were often held. Only twenty people showed up; they gathered around the speaker's table and had an uproarious discussion on political action *versus* Catholic Action. After that, Peter rented a small meeting room. The waste of money, laboriously collected, did not bother him. There was plenty of money in the world, he believed. What was needed was men absorbed by the right ideas. Given the men, the money would follow. All one needed to do was to pray. When bills piled up and creditors came, we used to go to church and pray, all of us taking turns, and we called this "the picketing of St. Joseph." Once when I asked an unemployed chambermaid if she would take a half-hour of "picketing Saint Joseph" over at Precious Blood Church, she asked me if she was to carry a sign. Once the printer sent us his bill with the notation, "Pray and pay!"

I asked Peter several times if he were not disappointed at the lack of success in indoctrinating the man on the street. I pointed to various examples of those who came to stay with us and whose condition seemed to get worse instead of better.

"People are just beginning to realize how deep-seated the evil is," he said soberly. "That is why we must be Catholic Radicals, we must get down to the roots. That is what radicalism is—the word means getting down to the roots."

Peter, even in his practicality, tried to deal with problems in the spirit of "the Prophets of Israel and the Fathers of the Church." He saw what the Industrial Revolution had done to the common man, and he did not think that unions and organizations, strikes for higher wages and shorter hours, were going to be the solution. "Strikes don't strike me," he used to say when we went out to a picket line to distribute literature during a strike. But he came with us to hand out the literature—leaflets which dealt with man's dignity and his need and right-to associate himself with his fellows in trade unions, in credit unions, cooperatives, maternity guilds, etc.

He was interested in far more fundamental approaches. He liked the name "radical" and he had wanted the paper to be called the *The Catholic Radical.* To him, *Worker* smacked of class war. What he wanted was to instill in all, worker or scholar, a philosophy of poverty and a philosophy of work.

He was the layman always. I mean that he never preached, he taught. While decrying secularism, the separation of the material from the spiritual, his emphasis, as a layman, was on man's material needs, his need for work, food, clothing and shelter. Though Peter went weekly to confession and daily to Communion and spent an hour a day in the presence of the Blessed Sacrament, his study was of the material order around him. Though he lived in the city, he urged a return to the village economy, the study of the crafts and of agriculture. He was dealing with this world, in which God has placed us to work for a new heaven and a new earth wherein justice dwelleth. Peter's idea of justice was that of Saint Thomas— to give each man what is his due.

He constantly urged individuals to practice the corporal and spiritual works of mercy; he urged Bishops to establish Houses of Hospitality. Somehow the two planks of the program got mixed up. I can remember well enough how it happened. He had written a series of essays addressed to the Bishops, pointing out to them that canon law called for the establishment of hospices in every bishopric. When a reader who had been sleeping in the subway came into *The Catholic Worker* office one day and disclosed her need (the apartment and the office were already full), Peter's literal acceptance of "If thy brother needs food or drink, feed him, and if he needs shelter, shelter him" meant that we rented a large apartment a block away which became the first House of Hospitality for women. This apartment expanded into three apartments and a store, then into a house, and finally into a twenty-room tenement house at 115 Mott Street. Eventually it included four additional apartments and two stores; then to become a double house at 223 Chrystie Street, New York City. Now we are in a loft on Spring Street, with eight apartments in the neighborhood. Here the works of mercy are still being practiced by the group who get out *The Catholic Worker*, living without salaries, in voluntary poverty. "Feeding thy brother" started with feeding a few poor men. It became a daily breadline in 1936, and the line still forms every day outside the door.

Round-table Discussions, Houses of Hospitality and Farming Communes—those were the three planks in Peter Maurin's platform. Despite war and re-employment which took many of our workers from us, there are still Houses of Hospitality, each autonomous but inspired by Peter, each trying to follow Peter's principles. And there are farms, all different but all starting with the idea of the personalist and communitarian revolution—to use Emmanuel Mounier's phrase. Peter was not disappointed in his life's work. He had given everything he had and he asked for nothing, least of all for success. He gave himself, and—at the end—God took from him the power to think.

He was docile and accepted his condition, though one could see the pain and struggle in his eyes. He, who had talked so much, became completely silent. For the last five years of his life he had to be served like a child, told when to go to bed, when to arise, what to eat, what to put on. He was the one led, rather than the leader.

He was anointed at Easton, Pennsylvania, for a bad heart condition, and a few years later, on May 15, 1949, he died at Maryfarm in Newburgh, New York. When his requiem was sung all the congregation who attended sang the Mass gloriously, triumphantly, joyously. Garbed in a donated suit of clothes, he was buried in a donated grave in St. John's Cemetery, Brooklyn.

Obituaries were found not only in *The Industrial Worker*, a Chicago I.W.W. paper which is on the subversive list, but also in *Osservatore Romano* in Vatican City, which carried its notice on the front page.

God has taken him into Paradise, with Lazarus who once was poor. May He bring us, too, to a place of refreshment, light and peace.

DOROTHY DAY

FOREWORD*

On May 1 *The Catholic Worker* celebrated its twenty-fifth birthday. It was on May Day in the midst of the depression, 1933, that the first issue of the famous penny paper was distributed free in Union Square. It was a historic day for the Church in America, for through the C.W.—which soon expanded from a paper into a movement— a vast amount of untapped Catholic energy was released.

Over the years some of this energy was undoubtedly misdirected to Utopian causes and half-baked schemes for remaking the world. But that sort of thing is inevitable when youthful idealism is engaged, as it always has been at the C.W. The *Worker*, which has existed for a quarter of a century without rules, regulations, memberships, committees or endowment and which has studiously rejected the techniques of organization and the counsels of worldly caution, has lasted longer than most of the soberly conceived undertakings which were begun about the same time. In any real accounting, it must be held up as a model of efficiency and genuine prudence. It did what it set out to do.

It set out to feed the hungry, clothe the naked, and house the homeless. It has done that day by day, hour by hour, for twenty-five years. It set out to get people talking and thinking about the things that really matter. It succeeded brilliantly here. It set out to recover the evangelical spirit and bear witness to the simplicities of the Gospel in the modern world. No one can equal its record in doing this. It set out to bring "scholar" and "worker"—in Peter Maurin's quaint classification—together. To a remarkable degree this program was a success.

From the beginning *The Catholic Worker* was pacifist-minded. That was the least remarkable thing about the paper when it first appeared, for in 1933 everyone talked like a pacifist. It was not until the Spanish Civil War, when the *Worker's* steadfastness

*Copyright *The Commonweal* May 16, 1958. Again this is a selection and condensation, approved by both author and publisher; and again most gratefully acknowledged.

was first tested, that pacifism became a major issue. By 1940 it had become the most controversial plank in the C.W. program, and it remains so today. But through war and peace the *Worker* has survived and for almost three decades now has never ceased to challenge the jingoism and patriotic extravagance found even in the Church. For years, whatever serious thinking was done about the moral problem of war was stimulated and in a perverse way encouraged by the C.W.'s insistence on nonresistance. I have long found it hard to take the paper very seriously on this question, because what it has to say has usually struck me as simplistic, evasive and even sentimental. But I am ready to admit that these very weaknesses may have been the *Worker's* great strength. Its position has been so extreme that it succeeded in making it impossible for nonpacifists like me to accept violence unthinkingly.

In the early days, *The Catholic Worker* used to talk about putting people back on the land and restoring an agrarian economy and way of life. Over the years there were heroic, sometimes quixotic, efforts made by groups and individuals to turn this part of the program into reality. Farming communes were actually established in several places. None of them turned out to be the model communities that Peter Maurin and Dorothy Day used to talk about so fervently, but a number of people seem to have found satisfaction and fulfillment in living according to their agrarian ideal.

Perhaps the *Worker,* for all of its haphazard methods, was so successful in what it set out to do because its ambitions were so modest and its pretensions so few. Dorothy Day always put a great deal of emphasis on the "little way" of a Saint Francis or a Thérése of Lisieux. Here, I suspect, is the secret of the abiding vitality found in the movement. It is not impressed by the grandiose. It has little respect for power. It is never nervously worrying about its own public relations. Paradoxically, in willingly, even joyously, giving up these things it has gained them.

By insisting on translating the grandeur of Christian theology into such simple terms as feeding the hungry or nursing the sick, it has not belittled theology but enhanced its appeal. Many a young person who comes to the *Worker* unlettered in theology ends up eagerly devouring Augustine, Thomas and Bonaventure. The movement which never sought power has had more influence on more influential Catholics than any other single force in the American Church.

JOHN COGLEY

PUBLISHER'S NOTE

In 1936 a small paperbacked selection of Peter Maurin's writings was published by Sheed and Ward, under the title EASY ESSAYS by Peter Maurin (with illustrations by Ade Bethune, 112 pp.). In August, 1949 a definitive collection of all of Peter Maurin's work was published as CATHOLIC RADICALISM: PHRASED ESSAYS FOR THE GREEN REVOLUTION by Catholic Worker books (213 pp., illustrations by Ed Willock). Both editions have been of print for some years.

The present volume—edited by Dorothy Day and the current editors of *The Catholic Worker*—is an attempt to present the essence of Peter Maurin's thought, in the versions he left at his death, with some of the repetitions "and the more ephemeral essays which had to do with Hitlerism, the NRA, etc.," deleted.

Some writers have claimed that at his death Peter Maurin left behind a considerable body of unpublished manuscript. Miss Day affirms that all of Peter Maurin's original writing was included in CATHOLIC RADICALISM —that any unpublished material which existed in Peter Maurin's handwriting at his death consisted solely of the condensations and paraphrases of other writers' work, in which he was engaged throughout his life.

Miss Day and the editors of *The Catholic Worker* believe that the present volume should represent the ultimate and authoritative edition of Peter Maurin's "Easy Essays."

The present publishers would like to acknowledge an especial debt to Mr. Fritz Eichenberg—who has made his lovely woodcuts as freely available to them as he has, for years, to *The Catholic Worker*.

CONTENTS

BOOK 1

EICHENBERG

BLOWING THE DYNAMITE

Writing about the Catholic Church,
a radical writer says:
"Rome will have to do more
than to play a waiting game;
she will have to use
some of the dynamite
inherent in her message."
To blow the dynamite
of a message
is the only way
to make the message dynamic.
If the Catholic Church
is not today
the dominant social dynamic force,
it is because Catholic scholars
have failed to blow the dynamite
of the Church.
Catholic scholars
have taken the dynamite
of the Church,
have wrapped it up
in nice phraseology,
placed it in an hermetic container
and sat on the lid.
It is about time
to blow the lid off
so the Catholic Church
may again become
the dominant social dynamic force.

OUT OF THE TEMPLE

Christ drove the money changers
out of the Temple.
But today nobody dares
to drive the money lenders
out of the Temple.
And nobody dares
to drive the money lenders
out of the Temple
because the money lenders
have taken a mortgage
on the Temple.

3

When church builders build churches
with money borrowed from money lenders
they increase the prestige
of the money lenders.
But increasing the prestige
of the money lenders
does not increase the prestige
of the Church.
Which makes Archbishop McNicholas say:
"We have been guilty
of encouraging tyranny
in the financial world
until it has become
a veritable octopus
strangling the life
of our people."

ETHICS AND ECONOMICS

Lincoln Steffens says:
"The social problem
is not a political problem;
it is an economic problem."
Kropotkin says:
"The economic problem
is not an economic problem;
it is an ethical problem."
Thorstein Veblen says:
"There are no ethics in modern society."
R. H. Tawney says:
"There were high ethics
in society
when the Canon Law
was the law of the land."
The high ethics
of the Canon Law
are embodied in the encyclicals
of Pius XI and Leo XIII
on the social problem.
To apply the ethics
of the encyclicals
to the problems of today,
such is the purpose
of Catholic Action.

THE MONEY LENDERS' DOLE

Uncle Sam does not believe
in the unemployed dole,
but Uncle Sam does believe
in the money lenders' dole.
Uncle Sam doles out every year
more than a billion dollars
to the money lenders.
And it is the money lenders' dole
that put Uncle Sam
into a hole.
The money lenders are first citizens
on Uncle Sam's payroll.
There were no money lenders
on the payroll
in Palestine and Ireland.
There were no money lenders
on the payroll
in Palestine and Ireland
because the Prophets of Israel
and the Fathers of the Church
forbid lending money at interest.
But Uncle Sam does not listen
to the Prophets of Israel
and the Fathers of the Church.

CREATING PROBLEMS

Business men say
that because everybody is selfish,
business must therefore
be based on selfishness.
But when business is based on selfishness
everybody is busy becoming more selfish.
And when everybody is busy
becoming more selfish,
we have classes and clashes.
Business cannot set its house in order
because business men are
moved by selfish motives.
Business men create problems,
they do not solve them.

WHEN CIVILIZATION DECAYS

When the bank account
is the standard of values

5

the class on the top
sets the standard.
When the class on the top
cares only for money
it does not care
for culture.
When the class on the top
does not care
for culture,
nobody cares
for culture.
And when nobody cares
for culture
civilization decays.
When class distinction
is not based
on the sense of *noblesse oblige,*
it becomes clothes distinction.
When class distinction
has become clothes distinction
everybody tries
to put up a front.

CHURCH AND STATE

Modern society believes
in separation
of Church and State.
But the Jews
did not believe in it,
the Greeks
did not believe in it,
the Medievalists
did not believe in it,
the Puritans
did not believe in it.
Modern society
has separated
the Church from the State,
but it has not separated
the State from business.
Modern society
does not believe
in a Church's State;

it believes
in a business men's State.
"And it is the first time
in the history of the world
that the State is controlled
by business men,"
says James Truslow Adams.

SELF-ORGANIZATION
People go to Washington,
asking the Federal Government
to solve their economic problems,
while the Federal Government
was never intended
to solve men's economic problems.
Thomas Jefferson says that
the less government there is,
the better it is.
If the less government there is,
the better it is,
then the best kind of government
is self-government.
If the best kind of government
is self-government,
then the best kind of organization
is self-organization.
When the organizers try
to organize the unorganized,
then the organizers
don't organize themselves.
And when the organizers
don't organize themselves,
nobody organizes himself,
And when nobody organizes himself,
nothing is organized.

*[An address by Peter
Maurin to the unem-
ployed at a meeting
held in September,
1933, at Manhattan
Lyceum, and pub-
lished in THE
CATHOLIC
WORKER, (October,
1933) in order that it
might be sent to all
the Bishops and Arch-
bishops meeting at
the National Confer-
ence of Catholic
Charities in New
York.]*

The Duty of Hospitality

People who are in need
and are not afraid to beg
give to people not in need
the occasion to do good
for goodness' sake.
Modern society calls the beggar
bum and panhandler
and gives him the bum's rush.
But the Greeks used to say
that people in need
are the ambassadors of the gods.
Although you may be called
bums and panhandlers
you are in fact the Ambassadors of God.
As God's Ambassadors
you should be given food,
clothing and shelter
by those who are able to give it.
Mahometan teachers tell us
that God commands hospitality,
and hospitality is still practiced
in Mahometan countries.
But the duty of hospitality
is neither taught nor practiced
in Christian countries.

The Municipal Lodgings

That is why you who are in need
are not invited to spend the night
in the homes of the rich.
There are guest rooms today
in the homes of the rich
but they are not for those who need them.
And they are not for those who need them
because those who need them
are no longer considered
as the Ambassadors of God.
So people no longer consider
hospitality to the poor
as a personal duty.
And it does not disturb them a bit

8

to send them to the city,
where they are given the
hospitality of the" Muni"
at the expense of the taxpayer.
But the hospitality that the
"Muni" gives to the down and out
is no hospitality
because what comes from the
taxpayer's pocketbook
does not come from his heart.

Back to Hospitality
The Catholic unemployed
should not be sent to the "Muni."
The Catholic unemployed
should be given hospitality
in Catholic Houses of Hospitality.
Catholic Houses of Hospitality
are known in Europe
under the name of hospices.
There have been hospices in Europe
since the time of Constantine.
Hospices are free guest houses;
hotels are paying guest houses.
And paying guest houses or hotels
are as plentiful
as free guest houses or hospices
are scarce.
So hospitality, like everything else,
has been commercialized.
So hospitality, like everything else,
must now be idealized.

Houses of Hospitality
We need Houses of Hospitality
to give to the rich
the opportunity to serve the poor.
We need Houses of Hospitality
to bring the Bishops to the people
and the people to the Bishops.
We need Houses of Hospitality
to bring back to institutions

9

the technique of institutions.
We need Houses of Hospitality
to show what idealism looks like
when it is practiced.
We need Houses of Hospitality
to bring social justice
through Catholic Action
exercised in Catholic institutions.

Hospices
We read in the *Catholic Encyclopedia*
that during the early ages of Christianity
the hospice (or the House of Hospitality)
was a shelter for the sick, the poor,
the orphans, the old, the traveler,
and the needy of every kind.
Originally the hospices (or
Houses of Hospitality)
were under the supervision of the Bishops,
who designated priests
to administer the spiritual
and temporal affairs
of these charitable institutions.
The fourteenth statute
of the so-called Council of Carthage,
held about 436,
enjoins upon the Bishops
to have hospices (or Houses of Hospitality)
in connection with their churches.

Parish Houses of Hospitality
Today we need Houses of Hospitality
as much as they needed them then,
if not more so.
We have Parish Houses for the priests,
Parish Houses for educational purposes,
Parish Houses for recreational purposes,
but no Parish Houses of Hospitality.
Bossuet says that the poor
are the first children of the Church,
so the poor should come first.
People with homes should

have a room of hospitality.
So as to give shelter
to the needy members
of the parish.
The remaining needy
members of the parish
should be given shelter in a Parish Home.
Furniture, clothing, and food
should be sent to the needy
members of the parish
at the Parish House of Hospitality.
We need Parish Homes
as well as Parish Domes.
In the new Cathedral of Liverpool
there will be a Home
as well as a dome.

Houses of "Catholic Action"
Catholic Houses of Hospitality
should be more than free guest houses
for the Catholic unemployed.
They could be vocational training schools,
including the training for the priesthood,
as Father Corbett proposes.
They could be Catholic reading rooms,
as Father McSorley proposes.
They could be Catholic Instruction Schools,
as Father Cornelius Hayes proposes.
They could be Round-Table
Discussion Groups,
as Peter Maurin proposes.
In a word, they could be
Catholic Action Houses,
where Catholic Thought
is combined with Catholic Action.

Dear Father:
In your instruction about writing
you told us that the best way
to learn to write
is to write letters
because a letter is a message
from someone to somebody
about something.
So this is a message
from an agitator to another agitator
about a discontented world
which begins to realize
that things are not good enough
to be left alone.
The Catholic Worker thinks
that you are a wonder.
We know what good work you are doing
among Catholic college youth.
But Catholic college youth
is a small proportion of Catholic youth
and all Catholic youth needs you.
Not only all Catholic youth needs you
but all youth needs you.
And not only all those who
are in their first youth
but all those who are getting
in their second youth
and also all those who have
reached the age of maturity
without having reached the
state of maturity.
That is to say,
we all need you.
We all need you
because you have the knack
of getting at the core of things
and of presenting your findings
in a vivid and dynamic form.

In one of his editorials Father Gillis says
that this age is very much like
the age of the fall of Rome

12

and that we could use one another
St. Augustine.
Father Gillis adds
that we need men to stir things up
and that we have too many
who try to smother them down.
You certainly can stir things up
and you can do that with
much ease.

It is said that Abbé Chardonnel,
who was a poet,
became a priest
so he could be more of a poet.
You, who are a born agitator,
have become a priest,
which makes you more of an agitator.
In St. Louis University
you turn out Masters of Arts,
but as Diego Rivera says:
"All art is propaganda."
And as all propaganda is agitation,
it behooves St. Louis University,
one of the best American universities,
to turn out Masters of Agitation.
So *The Catholic Worker* suggests
that you, our Master Catholic Agitator,
start in St. Louis University
a School of Catholic Agitation
for the popularization of Catholic Action.
Yours for Catholic Action,
For The Catholic Worker,
PETER MAURIN

To Be a Marxian

Before he died, Karl Marx
told one of his friends,
"I have lived long enough to
be able to say
that I am not a Marxian."
To be a Marxian, according to
the logic of *Das Kapital,*
is to maintain that the best thing to do
is to wait patiently till capitalism
has fulfilled its historic mission.
To be a Marxian, according to
the logic of *Das Kapital,*
is to step back, take an
academic view of things
and watch the self-satisfied capitalists
dig their own graves.
To be a Marxian, according to
the logic of *Das Kapital,*
is to have faith in the forces of
materialism—
forces so powerful, according
to materialists,
that they will bring the millennium
whether man wants it or not.
To be a Marxian, according to
the logic of *Das Kapital,*
is to let economic evolution do its work
without ever attempting to give it a push

What Karl Marx Realized

Karl Marx soon realized
that his own analysis of bourgeois society
could not be the basis
of a dynamic revolutionary movement.
Karl Marx soon realized
that a forceful Communist Manifesto
was the necessary foundation
of a dynamic Communist Movement.
Karl Marx soon realized,
as Lenin realized,

that there is no revolution
without revolutionary action,
that there is no revolutionary action
without a revolutionary movement,
that there is no revolutionary movement
without a vanguard of revolution,
and that there is no vanguard
of revolution
without a theory of revolution.

The Communist Manifesto
Having realized that a
Communist Manifesto
was the basis of a Communist Movement,
Karl Marx decided to write
a Communist Manifesto.
To write the Communist Manifesto
Karl Marx did not use his
analysis of capitalism.
He took the definition of
Communism of Proudhon
and made it his own.
He borrowed Utopian
criticism and Utopian aims
and decided to advocate class-struggle,
that is to say, materialist aims.
As some people used to think
that we need a good honest war
to end all wars,
Karl Marx used to think
that we need a gigantic class-struggle
to bring about a classless society.

For Catholic Action
We Catholics have a better criticism
of bourgeois society
than Victor Considerant's criticism,
used by Karl Marx.
Our criticism of bourgeois society
is the criticism of St. Thomas More.
We Catholics have a better
conception of Communism
than the conception of Proudhon.

Our conception of Communism
is the conception of St. Thomas Aquinas
in his doctrine of the "Common Good."
We Catholics have better means
than the means proposed by Karl Marx.
Our means to realize the "Common Good"
are embodied in Catholic Action.
Catholic Action is action by Catholics
for Catholics and non-Catholics.
We don't want to take over the control
of political and economic life.
We want to reconstruct the social order
through Catholic Action
exercised in Catholic
institutions.

The Bishops' Program
Shortly after the war
Bishops of America
formulated a Program of
Social Reconstruction
largely based on co-operation.
But the Bishops' Program
failed to materialize
for lack of co-operators.
Catholic laymen and women
were more interested
in a laissez-faire economy.
So Catholic laymen and women
went back to Normalcy with Harding;
they tried to Keep Cool with Coolidge,
and then to See Rosy with Roosevelt.
Catholic laymen and women
are more interested
in political action
than they are interested
in Catholic Action.
Catholic laymen and women
are more ready to follow
the leadership of the politicians
than they are ready to follow
the leadership of the Bishops.

Reconstructing the Social Order

The Holy Father and the Bishops ask us
to reconstruct the social order.
The social order was once constructed
through dynamic Catholic Action.
When the barbarians invaded
the decaying Roman Empire
Irish missionaries went all over Europe
and laid the foundations of medieval Europe.
Through the establishment of
cultural centers,
that is to say, Round-Table Discussions,
they brought thought to the people.
Through free guest houses,
that is to say, Houses of Hospitality,
they popularized the divine
virtue of charity.
Through farming colonies,
that is to say, Agronomic Universities,
they emphasized voluntary poverty.
It was on the basis of personal charity
and voluntary poverty
that Irish missionaries
laid the foundations
of the social order.

IS INFLATION INEVITABLE?

Usurers Not Gentlemen

The Prophets of Israel
and the Fathers of the Church
forbid lending money at interest.
Lending money at interest
is called usury
by the Prophets of Israel
and the Fathers of the Church.
Usurers were not considered
to be Gentlemen
when people used to listen
to the Prophets of Israel
and the Fathers of the Church.
When people used to listen
to the Prophets of Israel
and the Fathers of the Church

17

They could not see anything gentle
in trying to live
on the sweat of somebody else's brow
by lending money at interest.

Wealth-Producing Maniacs

When John Calvin
legalized moneylending
at interest
he made the bank account
the standard of values.
When the bank account
became the standard of values,
people ceased
to produce for use
and began
to produce for profits.
When people began
to produce for profits
they became
wealth-producing maniacs.
When people became
wealth-producing maniacs
they produced
too much wealth.
When people found out
that they had produced
too much wealth
they went on an orgy
of wealth destruction
and destroyed
ten million lives besides.
And fifteen years after
a world-wide orgy
of wealth and life
destruction
millions of people
find themselves victims
of a world-wide depression
brought about
by a world gone mad
on mass-production
and mass-distribution.

Legalized Usury

Because John Calvin legalized
money-lending at interest,
the State has legalized
money-lending at interest.
Because the State has legalized
money-lending at interest,
home-owners have mortgaged their homes.
Because the State has legalized
money-lending at interest,
farmers have mortgaged their farms.
Because the State has legalized
money-lending at interest,
institutions have mortgaged
their buildings.
Because the State has legalized
money-lending at interest,
congregations have
mortgaged their churches.
Because the State has legalized
money-lending at interest,
cities, counties, States,
and the Federal Government
have mortgaged their budgets.
So people find themselves
in all kinds of financial difficulties
because the State has legalized
money-lending at interest.

The Fallacy of Saving

When people save money,
they invest that money.
Money invested
increases production.
Increased production
brings a surplus
in production.
A surplus in production
brings unemployment.
Unemployment brings a slump
in business.
A slump in business

brings more unemployment.
More unemployment
brings a depression.
A depression
brings more depression.
More depression
brings red agitation.
Red agitation
brings red revolution.

Avoiding Inflation
Some say
that inflation
is desirable.
Some say
that inflation
is deplorable.
Some say
that inflation
is deplorable but inevitable.
The way
to avoid inflation
is to lighten the burden
of the money borrowers
without robbing
the money lenders.
And the way
to lighten the burden
of the money borrowers
without robbing
the money lenders
is to pass two laws,
one law
making immediately illegal
all interest
on money lent
and another law
obliging the money borrowers
to pay one per cent
of their debt
every year
during a period of a hundred years.

Dear Father:
There is a lot of talk today
about the social value of Fascism.
But Fascism is only a stopgap
between capitalism and Bolshevism.
Fascist dictatorship is a halfway house
between the rugged
individualism of capitalism
and the rugged collectivism of Bolshevism.
There is no essential difference
between Fascist dictatorship
and Bolshevik dictatorship.
The trouble with the world today
is too much dictatorship
and too little leadership.

Leadership cannot be found
among politicians, business men
and college professors.
The appointed leaders of mankind
are the Catholic Bishops.
Catholic Bishops have ceased to lead
because Catholic laymen and women
do not consider the Bishops
as their leaders
in political and economic matters.
Catholic laymen and women
look up to the Bishops
in spiritual matters
and look up to politicians and
business men
in political and economic matters.
Catholic laymen and women
commit the great modern error
of separating the spiritual
from the material.
This great modern error,
known under the name of secularism,
is called a "modern plague"
by Pope Pius XI.
You, who are a born agitator
and a theologian,

21

should bring a thorough understanding
between Bishops, clergy, and lay people.
From that understanding
would spring a form of Catholic Action
that would be dynamic in character.
We are threatened with
dynamic Bolshevik action
because we are sorely lacking
in dynamic Catholic Action.

PETER MAURIN

A RUMPUS ON THE CAMPUS

Two years ago
I went to see Professor Moley,
former head
of President Roosevelt's Brain Trust,
and said to him:
"I came here to find out
if I could make an impression
on the depression
by starting a rumpus
on the campus.
But I found out
that agitation is not rampant
on the campus.
Only business is rampant on the campus,
although business is the bunk.
"May be," said I,
"history cannot be made
on the campus."

And turning toward his secretary,
Professor Moley said:
"That's right,
we don't make history
on the campus,
we only teach it."
And because history is taught
but not made
on the campus of our universities,
the Catholic Worker
is trying to make history
on Union Square,
where people have nothing to lose.
A battle royal is raging
between East and West,
between stock speculators
and land speculators,
between money lenders
and money borrowers.
To go back to the gold standard,
as the so-called "sound
money" people propose,
is to favor the money lenders

23

at the expense of the money borrowers.
To increase the amount of currency,
as the mild inflationists propose,
is to favor the money borrowers
at the expense of the money lenders.
To devise schemes
so as to bring about a rise in prices
is to favor both money lenders
and money borrowers
at the expense of the consuming public.

We made the mistake
of running business on credit
and credit has run into debts
and debts are leading us
toward bankruptcy.
The Jews had a way
of wiping off the slate.
Every fifty years,
the year of the Jewish Jubilee,
all debts were liquidated.
But nobody,
not even the Jews,
proposes this old-time solution.
John Maynard Keynes,
the well-known English economist, says
that we ought to ask ourselves
if the medieval economists
were not sound
in condemning money-lending
at interest.

In his book
on *Religion and the Rise of Capitalism,*
R. H. Tawney,
another English economist,
points out
that at the base of our acquisitive society
we find legalized usury,
or lending money at interest.
Because the State has legalized
money-lending at interest,

in spite of the teachings
of the Prophets of Israel
and the Fathers of the Church,
home owners have mortgaged their homes,
farm owners have mortgaged their farms,
institutions have mortgaged
their buildings,
governments have mortgaged
their budgets.
So we are where we are
because the State has legalized
money-lending at interest
in spite of the teachings
of the Prophets of Israel
and the Fathers of the Church.
To go back to the teachings
of the Prophets of Israel
and the Fathers of the Church,
as I propose in my Easy Essays
in the current number of *The
Catholic Worker,*
would not do any injustice
to the money lenders
or the money borrowers
or the consuming public.
Money lenders would get their
money back,
money borrowers would find
their burdens lightened,
and the consuming public
would not have to pay the bill.
We would go back to the point
from which we should never have gone.
We would go back to the time
when no one was called a gentleman
who indulged in money-lending at interest.
We would go back to the time
when people could not see anything gentle
in trying to live on the sweat
of somebody else's brow
by lending money at interest.
Many people say

that we cannot go back,
but I say
neither can we go ahead,
for we are parked in a blind alley.
And when people are parked
in a blind alley
the only thing to do is to go back.
For when people lend money at interest
that money is invested.
Money invested
increases production.
Increased production
brings a surplus in production.
A surplus in production
brings unemployment.
Unemployment
brings a slump in business.
A slump in business
brings more unemployment.
More unemployment
brings more depression,
A depression
brings more depression,
More depression
brings red agitation.
Red agitation
brings red revolution.

COMING TO UNION SQUARE

Two yeas ago I went to see
college professors
and asked them to give me
the formulation of those universal concepts
embodied in the universal message
of universal universities
that will enable the common man
to create a universal economy.
But college professors were
too busy teaching subjects
to be interested in mastering situations.
College professors
were too interested
in academic matters

to be interested
in dynamic matters.
But now college professors realize
that they must be men of action
as well as men of thought—
that they must be dynamic
as well as academic,
and that Union Square
can teach something to college professors
as well as learning from college professors.

**SCHOLARS
AND BOURGEOIS**

The scholar has told the bourgeois
that a worker is a man for all that.
But the bourgeois has told the scholar
that a worker is a commodity for all that.
Because the scholar has vision,
the bourgeois calls him a visionary.
So the bourgeois laughs at the
scholar's vision
and the worker is left without vision.
And the worker left by the
scholar without vision
talks about liquidating
both the bourgeois and the scholar.
The scholars must tell the workers
what is wrong
with the things as they are.
The scholars must tell the workers
how a path can be made
from the things as they are
to the things as they should be.
The scholars must collaborate
with the workers
in making a path
from the things as they are
to the things
as they should be.
The scholars must become workers
so the workers may be scholars.

BUILDING CHURCHES

Henry Adams tells us in his
autobiography
that he could not get an education
in America,
because education implies
unity of thought
and there is no unity of
thought in America.
So he went to England
and found that England
was too much like America.
So he went to France
and found that France
was too much like England and America.
But in France he found the
Cathedral of Chartres
and from the Cathedral of
Chartres he learned
that there was unity of thought
in thirteenth-century France.

People who built the Cathedral
of Chartres
knew how to combine
cult, that is to say liturgy,
with culture, that is to say philosophy,
and cultivation, that is to say agriculture.

The Cathedral of Chartres is
a real work of art
because it is the real expression
of the spirit of a united people.
Churches that are built today
do not express the spirit of the people.
"When a church is built,"
a Catholic editor said to me,
"the only thing that has news value is:
How much did it cost?"
The Cathedral of Chartres was not built
to increase the value of real estate.
The Cathedral of Chartres was not built
with money borrowed from money lenders.

The Cathedral of Chartres was not built
by workers working for wages.

Maurice Barrés used to worry
about the preservation of
French Cathedrals,
but Charles Péguy thought
that the faith that builds Cathedrals
is after all the thing that matters.
Moscow had a thousand churches
and people lost the faith.
Churches ought to be built
with donated money, donated
material, donated labor.

The motto of St. Benedict was
Laborare et Orare, Labor and Pray.
Labor and prayer ought to be combined;
labor ought to be a prayer.
The liturgy of the Church
is the prayer of the Church.
People ought to pray with the Church
and to work with the Church.
The religious life of the people
and the economic life of the people
ought to be one.
I heard that in Germany
a group of Benedictines
is trying to combine liturgy
with sociology.
We don't need to wait for Germany
to point the way,
Architects, artists and artisans
ought to exchange ideas
on Catholic liturgy and Catholic sociology.

*[A reader in Belling-
ham, Wash., wrote to
Peter Maurin urging
the organization of
Catholic Labor Guilds
throughout the coun-
try. Members would
be assessed a dollar
a year, and the money
so raised would be
used to start Houses
of Hospitality. Peter's
reply follows. (Febru-
ary, 1934.)]*

Most organizations exist,
not for the benefit of the organized,
but for the benefit of the organizers.
When the organizers try to organize the
unorganized
they do not organize themselves.
If everybody organized himself,
everybody would be organized.
There is no better way to be
than to be
what we want the other fellow to be.
The money that comes from assessments
is not worth getting.
The money that is worth getting
is the money that is given for charity's sake.
Parish Houses of Hospitality
must be built on Christian charity.
But Parish Houses of Hospitality
are only half-way houses.
Parish Subsistence Camps
are the most efficient way
to make an impression
on the depression.
The basis for a Christian economy
is genuine charity and voluntary poverty.
To give money to the poor
is to increase the buying power of the poor.

Money is by definition a means of exchange
and not a means to make money.
When money is used as a means of exchange,
it helps to consume the goods that have been
produced.
When money is used as an investment,
it does not help to consume
the goods that have been produced,
it helps to produce more goods,
to bring over-production
and therefore increase unemployment.
So much money has been put into business
that it has put business out of business.

Money given to the poor is functional money.
money that fulfills its function.
Money used as an investment
is prostituted money,
money that does not fulfill its function.
Poverty and charity are no longer looked
up to,
they are looked down upon.
The poor have ceased to accept poverty
and the rich have ceased to practice charity.
When the poor are satisfied to be poor,
the rich become charitable toward the poor.

Because Christianity presents poverty as an
ideal
Bolshevik Communists try to make us believe
that religion is the opium of the people.
Karl Marx says that the worker is exploited
at the point of production.
But the worker would not be exploited
at the point of production
if the worker did not sell his labor
to the exploiter of his labor.

When the worker sells his labor
to a capitalist or accumulator of labor
he allows the capitalist or accumulator of
labor
to accumulate his labor.
And when the capitalist or accumulator of
the worker's labor
has accumulated so much of the worker's
labor
that he no longer finds it profitable
to buy the worker's labor
then the worker can no longer sell his labor
to the capitalist or accumulator of labor.
And when the worker can no longer sell his
labor
to the capitalist or accumulator of labor
he can no longer buy the products of his
labor.

And that is what the worker gets for selling
his labor
to the capitalist or accumulator of labor.
He just gets left
and he gets what is coming to him.
Labor is not a commodity
to be bought and sold—
Labor is a means of self-expression,
the worker's gift to the common good.

There is so much depression
because there is so little expression.
I am fostering Parish Subsistence Camps
or Agronomic Universities
as a means to bring about a state of society
where scholars are workers
and where workers are scholars.
In a Parish Subsistence Camp
or Agronomic University
the worker does not work for wages,
he leaves that to the University.
In a Parish Subsistence Camp
or Agronomic University
the worker does not look for a bank account
he leaves that to the University.
In a Parish Subsistence Camp
or Agronomic University
the worker does not look for an insurance
policy,
he leaves that to the University.
In a Parish Subsistence Camp
or Agronomic University
the worker does not look for an old-age
pension,
he leaves that to the University.
In a Parish Subsistence Camp
or Agronomic University
the worker does not look for a rainy day,
he leaves that to the University.
Modern industry has no work for everybody
but work can be found for everybody
in Parish Subsistence Camps

or Agronomic Universities.

I may later on publish a magazine entitled
The Agronomist
for the fostering of the idea
of Parish Subsistence Camps
or Agronomic Universities.
Edward Koch, of Germantown, Illinois,
publishes a magazine entitled
The Guildsman;
you ought to get in touch with him.
Your co-worker in Christ's Kingdom.
PETER MAURIN

PETER'S REPLY TO MICHAEL GUNN

[*Taking exception to Peter's answer to the Bellingham reader, Michael Gunn, oganizer of the Catholic Labor Guild in Brooklyn, wrote a critical letter, which drew the following reply. (March, 1934.)*]

Dear Mike:
In my answer to a reader
from Bellingham, Washington,
I said most organizations exist,
not for the benefit of the organized
but for the benefit of the organizers.
I added that when the organizers
try to organize the unorganized
they do not organize themselves.
When I wrote that
I did not have in mind
the Catholic Labor Guild in Brooklyn.
I had in mind
some selfish exploiters
of the exploitation of the exploited
who like to be called labor leaders.
I had in mind
some exalted rulers of secret societies
who, while they call themselves Masons,
have not yet learned
to create order out of chaos.
I had in mind
some dignified regulators
of societies which have some secrets
without being called secret societies.
While I don't like some of your ideas,
I like you personally.
I think that you are much better
than some of your ideas.

33

I think that you are inclined
to lead a life of sacrifice.
During the World War you placed your life
at the service of the British Empire.
After the war, you placed your life
at the service of the Irish Republic.
And now you have placed your life
at the service of the Church.
You and your fellow workers
of the Catholic Labor Guild
are trying to combine
prayer, action, and sacrifice,
as the Holy Father suggests.
You and your fellow workers
want to be go-givers,
you don't want to be go-getters.
Since you and your fellow workers
want to be go-givers,
you ought to give
to those who are in need of giving.
To give to people who have money to lend
is to give to people who are not in need.
People who have money
should do good with their money,
either give it away,
as our Saviour advises,
or lend it without interest.
To pay interest on money loaned
is to place an enterprise
under a too heavy burden.
Everyone must live on the sweat of his brow
and not on money loaned.
Nobody could lend money at interest
if nobody would borrow money at interest.
People who live on money loaned at interest
reap some of the profits of property
without the responsibility of property.
To pay double wages to managers
is to make the workers
envious of the managers.
Managers should receive what they need
and no more than they need.

Knowledge obliges as well as *"noblesse oblige."*
We cannot have a Catholic democracy
without a Catholic aristocracy.
Paying double wages to managers
is not the way to make aristocrats
out of efficient managers.
"The most important of all are Workmen's
Associations
and it is greatly to be desired
that they should multiply
and become more effective,"
says Pope Leo XIII.
To borrow money at interest
and to pay double wages to managers
is not absolutely necessary
to the good functioning
of Workmen's Associations.
You say that the Catholic Labor Guild
does not lend money at interest.
I hope that it will see the way
not to borrow money at interest.
You say that the Catholic Labor Guild
stands for profit-sharing.
I hope that your self-sacrificing example
will lead the members of the Guild
to stand for loss-sharing.
When the members of the Guild
decide to allow the Guild
to accumulate the profits
they will not need to worry
about their economic security.
Let the members of the Guild
give all they can to the Guild;
the Guild will not leave them in want.
Let the Labor Guild help
all those it can help
and the Farming Communes will help
all those that the Guild cannot help.
Yours for Catholic Action.
PETER MAURIN

35

Program

The purpose of the Catholic Workers' School
is to bring Cotholic thought
to Catholic workers
so as to prepare them
for Catholic Action.
Besides presenting Catholic thought
to Catholic workers
the Catholic Workers' School
presents a program of Catholic Action
based on Catholic thought.
The program of the Catholic Workers'
School
is a three-point program:
1. Round-table Discussions
2. Houses of Hospitality
3. Farming Communes.

Round-Table Discussions

We need Round-Table Discussions
to keep trained minds from being academic.
We need Round-Table Discussions
to keep untrained minds from being superficial.
We need Round-Table Discussions
to learn from scholars
how things would be,
if they were as they should be.
We need Round-Table Discussions
to learn from scholars
how a path can be made
from things as they are
to things as they should be.

Communes

We need Communes
to help the unemployed
to help themselves.
We need Communes
to make scholars out of workers
and workers out of scholars,
to substitute a technique of ideals
for our technique of deals.
We need Communes

to create a new society
within the shell of the old
with the philosophy of the new,
which is not a new philosophy
but a very old philosophy,
a philosophy so old
that it looks like new.

Catholic Social Philosophy
The Catholic social philosophy
is the philosophy of the Common Good
of St. Thomas Aquinas.
Three books where this philosophy is
expressed are:
*The Thomistic Doctrine of the Common
Good,* by Seraphine Michel;
The Social Principles of the Gospel,
by Alphonse Lugan;
Progress and Religion, by Christopher
Dawson.

THE CASE FOR UTOPIA

Better and Better Off
The world would be better off
if people tried to become better.
And people would become better
if they stopped trying to become better off.
For when everybody tries to become
better off,
nobody is better off.
But when everybody tries to become better,
everybody is better off.
Everybody would be rich
if nobody tried to become richer.
And nobody would be poor
if everybody tried to be the poorest.
And everybody would be what he ought
to be
if everybody tried to be
what he wants the other fellow to be.

Christianity has nothing to do
with either modern capitalism
or modern Communism,

for Christianity has
a capitalism of its own
and a communism of its own.
Modern capitalism
is based on property without responsibility,
while Christian capitalism
is based on property with responsibility.
Modern Communism
is based on poverty through force
while Christian communism
is based on poverty through choice.
For a Christian,
voluntary poverty is the ideal
as exemplified by St. Francis of Assisi,
while private property
is not an absolute right, but a gift
which as such can not be wasted,
but must be administered
for the benefit of God's children.

According to Johannes Jörgensen,
a Danish convert living in Assisi,
St. Francis desired
that men should give up
superfluous possessions.
St. Francis desired
that men should work with their hands.
St. Francis desired
that men should offer their services
as a gift.
St. Francis desired
that men should ask other people for help
when work failed them.
St. Francis desired
that men should live
as free as birds.
St. Francis desired
that men should go through life
giving thanks to God for His gifts.

Three Ways to Make a Living
Mirabeau says "There are three ways
to make a living:

Stealing, begging, and working."
Stealing is against the law of God
and against the law of men.
Begging is against the law of men
but not against the law of God.
Working is neither against the law of God
nor against the law of men.
But they say
that there is no work to do.
There is plenty of work to do,
but no wages.
But people do not need to work for wages,
they can offer their services as a gift.

Capital and Labor
"Capital," says Karl Marx, "is accumulated
labor,
not for the benefit of the laborers,
but for the benefit of the accumulators."
And capitalists succeed in accumulating
labor,
by treating labor, not as a gift,
but as a commodity,
buying it as any other commodity
at the lowest possible price.
And organized labor plays into the hands
of the capitalists, or accumulators of labor,
by treating its own labor
not as a gift, but as a commodity,
selling it as any other commodity
at the highest possible price.
And the class struggle is a struggle
between the buyers of labor
at the lowest possible price
and the sellers of labor
at the highest possible price.
But the buyers of labor
at the lowest possible price
and the sellers of labor
at the highest possible price
are nothing but commercializers of labor.

Selling Their Labor

When the workers
sell their labor
to the capitalists
or accumulators of labor
they allow the capitalists
or accumulators of labor
to accumulate their labor.
And when the capitalists
or accumulators of labor
have accumulated so much
of the workers' labor
that they do no longer
find it profitable
to buy the workers' labor
then the workers
can no longer sell their labor
to the capitalists
or accumulators of labor.
And when the workers
can no longer
sell their labor
to the capitalists
or accumulators of labor
they can no longer buy
the products of their labor.
And that is what the workers get
for selling their labor.

THE BISHOPS' MESSAGE— QUOTATIONS AND COMMENTS

[These excerpts from the Bishops' Message of 1934, with Peter Maurin's comments, were published in the Catholic Worker of May, 1934. The quo-

In tracing the remote causes
of the present misery of mankind
we must listen to him
who as a loving father
views from an eminence
all the nations of the world.
Quoting St. Paul, our Holy Father says:
"The desire for money
is the root of all evil."
From greed arises mutual distrust
that casts a blight
on all human beings.

*tations are printed
here in Roman type
and Peter's comments
in italics.]*

From greed arises envy
which makes a man
consider the advantages of another
as losses to himself.
From greed arises
narrow individualism
which orders and subordinates everything
to its own advantage.

*People looking
for a rainy day
have put so much money
into business
that they have brought about
an increase
in producing power
and a decrease
in purchasing power.
So there is a rub
between the rich
who like
to get richer
and the poor
who don't like
to get poorer.*

In common with other nations
we have brought about our present
unhappy conditions
by divorcing education, industry, politics,
business, and economics
from morality and religion
and by ignoring for long decades
the innate dignity of man
and trampling on his human rights.

*We have taken religion
out of everything
and have put commercialism
into everything.*

That we are an industrial nation

is our public boast.
Industry is considered to be of more importance
than the moral welfare of man.
The lord of all is Industry.
"Save Industry!" is the cry.
"Put business on its feet
and all will be well
as it was in the past."

We are beginning to learn
that to put big business
on its feet
does not necessarily
put the forgotten man
on his feet.

The philosophy which has ruled governments, groups, and individuals
for the past three hundred years
has not taken as its guide
the moral law,
has not considered the rights of men.
Money, not men,
has been the supreme consideration
and the justifying end.

When people care
for money
they do not care
for culture.
And when people
do not care
for culture
they return
to barbarism.

That philosophy permits individuals
to accumulate as much wealth as they can
according to unfair methods
of modern business
and to use such accumulated wealth

as they see fit.
This extreme of individualism
has led to the extreme of Communism.
We rightly fear its spread in our country
and see an especial menace
in its insidious presentation
of fundamental troubles
for its own destructive ends.

When modern society
made the bank account
the standard of values
people ceased
to produce for use
and began
to produce for profit.
Rugged individualism
leads to
rugged nationalism,
which leads to
rugged collectivism.

The brotherhood of man
is loudly proclaimed.
Energetic protest is made
against injustice
done to the working class.
The abuses of the capitalist system
are vigorously condemned.
It is insisted
that man shall not exploit his fellow man
and that all shall be dedicated
to a life of service.

In a capitalist society
where man
is inhuman to man
people cannot
keep from dreaming
about a society
where man
would be human
to man.

A program of social reform
couched in such language
and with such aims and purposes
is unassailable
because it is distinctly Christian in origin
and purport,
but in the hands of the Communists
it is merely a snare
to allure those who are oppressed
by the prevailing economic maladjustment
into accepting the iniquitous social and
religious tenets
of Lenin and Stalin.
There is a very grave and subtle danger
of infection from Communism.

According to St. Thomas Aquinas
man is more
than an individual
with individual rights;
he is a person
with personal duties
toward God,
himself,
and his fellow man.
As a person
man cannot
serve God
without serving
the Common Good.

Special efforts are being made
to win Negroes
who are the victims of injustice.
The Communists have as their objective
a world war on God
and the complete destruction
of all supernatural and even natural religion.

The Negroes
are beginning to find out

that wage slavery
is no improvement
on chattel slavery.
The Communists say
that Christianity is a failure,
but it is not a failure
for the very good reason
that it has not been tried.

TRADITION OR CATHOLIC ACTION

The central act of devotional life
in the Catholic Church
is the Holy Sacrifice of the Mass.
The Sacrifice of the Mass
is the unbloody repetition
of the Sacrifice of the Cross.
On the Cross of Calvary
Christ gave His life to redeem the world.
The life of Christ was a life of sacrifice.
The life of a Christian must be
a life of sacrifice.
We cannot imitate the sacrifice of Christ
on Calvary
by trying to get all we can.
We can only imitate the sacrifice of Christ
on Calvary
by trying to give all we can.

BOOK 2

**BIG SHOTS
AND LITTLE SHOTS**

America is all shot to pieces
since the little shots
are no longer able
to become big shots.
When the little shots
are not satisfied
to remain little shots
and try to become
big shots,
then the big shots
are not satisfied
to remain big shots
and try to become
bigger shots.
And when the big shots
become bigger shots
then the little shots
become littler shots.
And when the little shots
become littler shots
because the big shots
become bigger shots
then the little shots
get mad at the big shots.
And when the little shots
get mad at the big shots
because the big shots
by becoming bigger shots
make the little shots
littler shots
they shoot the big shots
full of little shots.
But by shooting the big shots
full of little shots
the little shots
do not become big shots;
they make everything all shot.
And I don't like
to see the little shots
shoot the big shots
full of little shots;
that is why

I am trying to shoot
both the big shots
and the little shots
full of hot shots.

A Modern Plague
Glenn Frank,
president of Wisconsin University,
says:
"What ails modern society
is the separation of the spiritual from the
material."
Pope Pius XI
calls this separation
"a modern plague,"
or to speak more plainly "a pest."
This separation of the spiritual from the
material
is what we call "secularism."
Everything has been secularized,
everything has been divorced from religion.
We have divorced religion from education,
we have divorced religion from politics,
we have divorced religion from business.

Secularism
When religion has nothing to do with
education,
education is only information,
plenty of facts
and no understanding.
When religion has nothing to do with
politics,
politics is only factionalism—
"Let's turn the rascals out
so our good friends can get in."
When religion has nothing to do with
business
business is only commercialism.
And when religion has nothing to do with
either education, politics or business,
you have the religion of business taking the
place of the business of religion.

50

Spiritualizing

Our modern educators,
our modern politicians,
our modern business men
have taken religion from everything
and have put commercialism into everything.
And now we have to take commercialism out
of everything
and to put religion into everything.
The way to take commercialism out of
everything
and to put religion into everything
is not through political action.
The way to take commercialism out of
everything
and to put religion into everything
is through Catholic Action.

Business-Like

Catholic Action is action by Catholics
for Catholics and non-Catholics.
Catholic Action is action by Catholic laymen
in co-operation with the clergy.
Catholic laymen and women have told
the clergy,
"Mind your own business
and don't butt into our business."
So Catholic clergymen
have ceased to mind the layman's business
and the laymen have made a mess
of their own business.
And Catholic clergymen have tried to mind
their business
with a business-like technique
borrowed from business-minded people.

The Forgotten Man

The forgotten man has been forgotten
because clergymen have forgotten
to rub shoulders with the forgotten man.
And clergymen have forgotten

to rub shoulders with the forgotten man
because clergymen have forgotten
to use logic to find what is practical.
And because clergymen have forgotten
to use logic to find what is practical
they have failed to give us a sociology
that has something to do with theology.
If there was a sociology
that had something to do with theology
it was the sociology of St. Francis of Assisi,
St. Thomas Aquinas and St. Thomas More.
But the sociology of St. Francis of Assisi,
St. Thomas Aquinas and St. Thomas More.
was an Utopian sociology,
and clergymen are not interested in Utopias,
not even Christian Utopias.

Rome or Moscow
And because clergymen are not interested
in the sociology of St. Francis of Assisi,
St. Thomas Aquinas and St. Thomas More,
the forgotten man is becoming interested
in the sociology of Karl Marx, Lenin
and Stalin.
And because clergymen are not interested
in a technique of leadership
the forgotten man is becoming interested
in a technique of dictatorship.
And because clergymen are not interested
in Dynamic Catholic Action
the forgotten man is becoming interested
in Dynamic Bolshevik Action.

COMMUNIST ACTION IN SCHOOLS A CHALLENGE TO CATHOLICS

I Was Told
I was told
by a young Puerto Rican
that the president
of his school's study club
was a Communist,
and that in the meetings
of the school's study club
the Communist president

did most of the talking
and that the school teacher
was an interested listener
to the Communist president
of the school's study club.
I was told
by the dean of a Catholic college
that Catholic professors
of Catholic colleges
have neither
the knowledge nor the courage
to bring Catholic social thought
to the man of the street.

Looking For Light
So while Catholic professors
of Catholic colleges
do not have
enough knowledge or courage
to bring Catholic social thought
to the man of the street,
Communist propagandists
yet in their 'teens
find enough knowledge or courage
to bring Communist social thought
to the men of the school.
The schools used to teach:
"If you want peace
prepare for war";
we prepared for war
and are still looking for peace.
The schools used to teach:
"If you want prosperity
save your money";
people saved their money,
and we are still looking for prosperity.
The modern man looks for thought
so he can have light,
and is unable to find it
in our modern schools.

Shouting With Rotarians

According to Glenn Frank,
president of the University of Wisconsin,
"Schools reflect the environment,
they do not create it."
According to Professor Meiklejohn,
of the same university,
students go to school
not to be educated,
but to be business men.
Shortly after their graduation
school graduates can be heard
shouting with Rotarians:
"Service for profits,
Time is money,
Cash and carry,
Keep smiling,
Business is business,
Watch your step,
How is the rush?
How are you making out?
How is the world treating you?
The law of supply and demand,
Competition is the life of trade,
Your dollar is your best friend."

A Protestant Agitator

Catholic teachers
teaching in Catholic or public schools
who do not know how to present
Catholic social thought
either to the men on the street
or to the pupils in the schools
will be interested to learn
that a Protestant agitator
well known in Union Square
is presenting the Thomistic doctrine
of the Common Good
to the men of the street
in the streets of Harlem.
H. Hergenhan, such is his name,
does not believe

in the rugged individualism
of capitalism
or in the rugged nationalism
of Fascism
or in the rugged collectivism
of Bolshevism.

The Common Good

He believes in the gentle personalism
of gentlemen who are gentle,
gentleness that finds its roots
in the common doctrine
of the Common Good.
H. Hergerhan believes
that the doctrine of the Common Good
is common
to humanists who are human,
to Jews who are orthodox,
to Protestants who are Christian
and to Catholics who are Catholic.
The Common Good movement
is not a movement that divides,
it is a movement that unites.
The Common Good movement
is not a new deal,
it is an old game.
The Common Good movement
is not a revolution to the left,
it is a revolution to the right.

Tawney's Book

When in 1891 Pope Leo XIII
wrote his encyclical
on the condition of labor
he emphasized the lack of ethics
in modern society.
When in 1899 Thorstein Veblen
wrote *The Theory of the Leisure Class*
he emphasized the same thing.
R. H. Tawney, then an Oxford student,
learned that when the Canon Law,

that is to say, the law of the Church,
was the law of the land
there were high ethics in society.
So R. H. Tawney decided to study
how society has passed down
from the high ethics of the Canon Law
to the no ethics of today.
What R. H. Tawney found out
about the history of ethics
of the last five hundred years
is embodied in his book,
Religion and the Rise of Capitalism.

SOCIAL STUDY SCHOOLS NEEDED

Catholic Social Research
"When a system fails to feed the poor
it is time to look out
for one that does,"
says Archbishop Keating of Liverpool.
And because Archbishop Keating realized
that our modern social order
fails to feed the poor
he founded in Oxford
a Catholic Labor College.
And the Catholic Labor College
conducted in Oxford
has been going on
for the last twenty-five years.
At its last general meeting
Cardinal Bourne declared
that we are badly in need
of Catholic social research.
If there had been more Catholic social
research
Catholics would not now
pass the buck
to the politicians.

School of Social Studies
To found a School of Social Studies,
such was the aim
of Father Patrick Sheely, S.J.
In a School of Social Studies

we would be able to learn
why things are what they are.
In a School of Social Studies
we would be able to learn
how things would be
if they were as they should be.
In a School of Social Studies
we would be able to learn
how a path can be made
from things as they are
to things as they should be.
A School of Social Studies
would give us Catholic Action
based on Catholic Thought
realized in Catholic Institutions.

Putting Patches
Having no School of Social Studies,
we don't know how to pass
from things as they are
to things as they should be.
Having no School of Social Studies
we have no Catholic social program
based on Catholic social thought.
Having no School of Social Studies,
we try to put patches
to the existing social order
and call it a New Deal.
Having no School of Social Studies,
we let college professors
carry on costly experiments
at the expense of the taxpayers.
Having no School of Social Studies,
we are not occupied
in reconstructing the social order
as the Holy Father wants us to be.

I Agree
I agree with seven Bishops,
three of whom are Archbishops,
that the Communist criticism
of modern rugged individualism

is a sound criticism.
I agree with seven Bishops,
three of whom are Archbishops,
that the main social aim
of the Communist Party
is a sound social aim.
I agree with seven Bishops,
three of whom are Archbishops,
that the Communists are not sound
when they advocate class struggle
in order to realize
their sound social aim.
I agree with the Apostolic Delegate
when he advocates the practice
of the Seven Corporal and Seven Spiritual
Works of Mercy
as the best practical means
of making man human to man.

Personal Sacrifice

To be our brother's keeper
is what God wants us to do.
To feed the hungry
at a personal sacrifice
is what God wants us to do.
To clothe the naked
at a personal sacrifice
is what God wants us to do.
To shelter the homeless
at a personal sacrifice
is what God wants us to do.
To instruct the ignorant
at a personal sacrifice
is what God wants us to do.
To serve man for God's sake
is what God wants us to do.

Reconstruction

The Holy Father asks us
to reconstruct the social order.
The social order was once reconstructed
after the fall of the Roman Empire.

The Irish scholars were the leaders
in the reconstruction of the social order
after the fall of the Roman Empire.
Through Round-Table Discussions
scattered all over Europe
as far as Constantinople
the Irish scholars
brought thought to the people.
Through Houses of Hospitality
the Irish scholars
exemplified Christian charity.
Through Farming Communes
the Irish scholars
made workers out of scholars
and scholars out of workers.

A THIRD OPEN LETTER TO FATHER LORD, S.J.

Dear Father:
Dr. C. Roper, Secretary of Commerce,
suggested some time ago
the establishment in Washington
of a "Laboratory for Leadership in
Public Affairs."
H. McCall, assistant to Secretary Roper
says that "youth movements
have occupied
dominant and aggressive positions
in the social and governmental changes
that have taken place
throughout the world
since the World War."
H. McCall proposes
the establishment in Washington
"of a forum
for study and training
in public affairs."

Colleges and universities
have failed
to give their students
a technique of leadership
based on scholarship.

And because colleges and universities
have failed
to make leaders out of their students,
politicians propose
to make bureaucrats out of them.
College professors
have become so academic
that their students
refuse to be scholarly minded
and consent to be politically minded.
College professors
have failed
to train their students
in a technique of leadership,
so their students wish to be trained
in a technique of dictatorship.
In Cuba, Germany, China, Mexico, Italy,
Russia, dictators have found
their greatest support
among college students
eager for action.
Academic college professors
are interested in thought,
not in action.
So we have on one hand
thought without action
and on the other hand
action without thought.

People go to Washington
asking the Federal Government
to solve their economic problems,
while the Federal Government
was never intended
to solve men's economic problems.
Catholic Action
based on Catholic thought
is the Catholic solution
of men's economic problems.
To impart Catholic thought
and train in Catholic Action,
such is the function

of Catholic universities.
Some way ought to be found
to send Catholic workers
to Catholic universities
or to bring Catholic universities
to Catholic workers.
When Catholic scholars
and Catholic workers
become acquainted with each other
Catholic workers
will cease to be politically minded
and begin to be scholarly minded.
When Catholic scholars
are dynamic
and not academic
and Catholic workers
are scholars
and not politicians
we will have dynamic Catholic Action.
Yours for dynamic Catholic Action,
PETER MAURIN

WHEN CHRIST IS KING

Not a Liberal

They say that I am a radical.
If I am a radical
then I am not a liberal.
The future will be different
if we make the present different.
But to make the present different
one must give up old tricks
and start to play new tricks.
But to give up old tricks
and start to play new tricks
one must be a fanatic.
Liberals are so liberal about everything
that they refuse to be fanatical
about anything.
And not being able to be fanatical
about anything,
liberals cannot be liberators.
They can only be liberals.

Liberals refuse to be
religious, philosophical or economic fanatics
and consent to be
the worst kind of fanatics,
liberal fanatics.

Not a Conservative
If I am a radical,
then I am not a conservative.
Conservatives try to believe
that things are good enough
to be let alone.
But things are not good enough
to be let alone.
Conservatives try to believe
that the world is getting better
every day in every way.
But the world is not getting better
every day in every way.
The world is getting worse
every day in every way
and the world is getting worse
every day in every way
because the world is upside down.
And conservatives do not know
how to take the upside down
and to put it right side up.
When conservatives and radicals
will come to an understanding
they will take the upside down
and they will put it right side up.

A Radical Change
The order of the day
is to talk about the social order.
Conservatives would like
to keep it from changing
but they don't know how.
Liberals try to patch it
and call it a New Deal.
Socialists want a change,
but a gradual change.

Communists want a change,
an immediate change,
but a Socialist change.
Communists in Russia
do not build Communism,
they build Socialism.
Communists want to pass
from capitalism to Socialism
and from Socialism to Communism.
I want a change,
and a radical change.
I want a change
from an acquisitive society
to a functional society,
from a society of go-getters
to a society of go-givers.

When Bankers Rule

Modern society has made the bank account
the standard of values.
When the bank account
becomes the standard of values
the banker has the power.
When the banker has the power
the technician has to supervise
the making of profits.
When the banker has the power
the politician
has to assure law and order
in the profit-making system.
When the banker has the power
the educator trains students
in the technique of profit making.
When the banker has the power
the clergyman is expected
to bless the profit-making system
or to join the unemployed.
When the banker has the power
the Sermon on the Mount
is declared unpractical.
When the banker has the power

we have an acquisitive,
not a functional society.

When Christ Is King
When the Sermon on the Mount
is the standard of values
then Christ is the Leader.
When Christ is the Leader
the priest is the mediator.
When Christ is the Leader
the educator
trains the minds of the pupils
so that they may understand
the message of the priest.
When Christ is the Leader
the politician
assures law and order
according to the priest's teachings.
When Christ is the Leader
the technician
devises ways and means
for the economical production
and distribution of goods.
When Christ is the Leader
the administrator administrates
according to the directions
from the technicians.
When Christ is the Leader
we have a functional,
not an acquisitive society.

Rebellion Is Rebellion
Boloney is boloney,
no matter how you slice it,
and rebellion is rebellion
no matter when it happens,
whether it is
the religious rebellion
of the 16th century
or the political rebellion
of the 18th century,
or the economic rebellion

of the 20th century.
Someone said
that the Catholic Church
stands for rum, Romanism and rebellion.
But the Catholic Church
does not stand for rum, Romanism and
rebellion.
The Catholic Church stands
for Rome, Reunion, and Reconstruction.
The Catholic Church stands,
as Rome used to stand,
for law and order.
The Catholic Church stands
for the reunion
of our separated brothers.
The Catholic Church stands
for the reconstruction,
not the patching up,
of the social order.

Constructing the Social Order

The Holy Father asks us
to reconstruct the social order.
The social order was constructed
by the first Christians
through the daily practice
of the Seven Corporal
and Seven Spiritual
Works of Mercy.
To feed the hungry
at a personal sacrifice,
to clothe the naked
at a personal sacrifice,
to shelter the homeless
at a personal sacrifice,
to instruct the ignorant
at a personal sacrifice;
such were the works
of the first Christians
in times of persecution.

The Catholic Worker proposes fighting
Communism
the way the first Christians
fought pagan Romanism,
through the works of mercy.
The Catholic Worker proposes fighting
Communism
the way the Irish scholars
fought pagan feudalism,
through Round-Table Discussions,
Houses of Hospitality,
Farming Communes.
The Communists do not build Communism,
they build Socialism.
The Catholic Worker
does not build Catholic Socialism,
it builds Catholic Communism.
The Catholic Worker
builds Catholic Communism
the way the first Christians
and the Irish scholars
built Catholic Communism.
The Catholic Worker believes
that there is no better Communism
than Catholic Communism,
and that there is no better way
to build Catholic Communism
than by building Catholic Communes.
Catholic Communes
are not a new thing,
they are an old thing.
Catholic Communes are so old
that Catholics have forgotten them.
Communists have not invented anything,
not even the name Commune.
The Communist ideal
is the Common Good ideal—
the ideal of St. Thomas More,
the ideal of St. Thomas Aquinas,
the ideal of the Irish scholars,
the ideal of the first Christians.

The doctrine of the Common Good
of St. Thomas Aquinas
is still a Catholic doctrine.
We don't need a new doctrine,
we need an old technique.
We need the old technique
of the first Christians
and the Irish scholars.
What was good for the first Christians
and the Irish scholars
ought to be good enough for us.
What was practical for them
ought to be practical for us.

Not Communists

There is nothing wrong
with Communism,
but there is something wrong
with Bolshevism.
The wrong thing with Bolshevism is
that Bolshevists
are not Communists;
they are Socialists.
For if the Bolshevists
were Communists,
they would build Communism.
And the Bolshevists
do not build Communism;
they build Socialism;
they build State Socialism.
The Bolshevists probably hope
that the State
"will wither away,"
and that they will be able to pass
from State Socialism
to Communism without State.

Two Reds

Some time ago
I was discussing in Harlem
with a Russian Red
and an Irish Red.
And the Russian Red
understood me sooner
than the Irish Red.
Having understood
what I was saying,
the Russian Red
started to explain
to his friend, the Irish Red,
what I was talking about.
When the Russian Red
had finished explaining,
the Irish Red

turned toward me
and said that while he agreed
with most of what I said
he still believed
that the Catholic Church
was not the friend
of the working-men.
Many Catholics
are much disappointed
when Wall Street corporations
or political organizations
or Catholic associations
fail to provide them
with economic security.

Looking for a Boss

A Catholic working-man
once said to me:
"There is only one thing
between me and the Reds,
and that is a good job."
Everybody is looking for a boss,
and nobody wants
to be his own boss.
And because everybody
looks for a boss
the Reds want the State
to be the boss of everybody.
Because everybody
consents to play
somebody else's game
for the sake of a pay-envelope
the Reds try to find the way
to assure a pay envelope
to everybody
so as to force everybody
to act like everybody.
But nothing will be changed
when the Reds
will force everybody
to act like everybody,
since nobody is nobody

when everybody
tries to keep up with everybody.

America and Russia
American Republicans
want their friends
on the public payroll,
but only *their* friends.
American Democrats
want their friends
on the public payroll,
but only *their* friends.
But the Reds want everybody
on the public payroll,
not only their friends.
The American idea
is to keep the Government
out of business
and to put everybody
into business.
The Russian idea
is to put the Government
into business
and to keep everybody
out of business.
But business
is only business,
whether it is
the State business
or private business;
and I am trying
to make it my business
to put all business
out of business,
including the State business,
which is a big business.

Red and Green
Our business managers
have made such a mess of things
that people are inclined
to see Red.

And when people see Red
it is useless
to present to them
the Red, White and Blue,
because they can no longer see
the White and the Blue
of the Red, White and Blue;
all they can see is Red.
The only way
to keep people
from seeing Red
is to make them
see Green.
The only way
to prevent
a Red Revolution
is to promote
a Green Revolution.
The only way
to keep people
from looking up
to Red Russia
of the twentieth century
is to make them look up
to Green Ireland.
of the seventh century.

Thousand Years Ago

When Irish were Irish
a thousand years ago,
the Irish were scholars.
And when the Irish were scholars
the Irish were Greek scholars.
And when the Irish were Greek scholars
the Irish spoke Greek
as well as Irish.
And when the Irish spoke Greek
as well as Irish,
Greek was Irish
to the Irish.
Greek was Irish
to the Irish

and now
Irish is Greek
to the Irish.
Irish is Greek
to the Irish now
and Hebrew is Chinese
to the Jews.

Social Missionaries

A School of Social Studies
would be the training ground
for Social Missionaries,
priests, laymen and women.
As Al Smith said:
"The social problem
is not a problem
for politicians,
business men,
and lawyers."
The social problem
is a problem
for Social Missionaries.
The task of Social Missionaries
is not to help people
to adjust themselves
to the existing environment.
The task of Social Missionaries
is to teach people
the difficult art
of creating order
out of chaos.
To be a Social Missionary
requires social-mindedness,
historical-mindedness
and practical idealism.

Study Clubs

Social Missionaries
would be official leaders
of Study Clubs.
The conduct of a Study Club
does not require

a fluent speaker.
As Bishop O'Hara said:
"The purpose of Study Clubs
is to make people articulate;
and lectures do not help
to make people articulate."
Social Missionaries
would be able
to impart their knowledge
through easy conversations.
Easy conversations
about things that matter
would keep people
from going to the movies,
from talking politics,
from cheap wisecracking.
Easy conversation
about things that matter
would enable Catholics
to understand Catholicism,
to give an account of their faith,
and to make non-Catholics
curious about Catholicism.

Works of Mercy
The best kind of apologetics
is the kind of apologetics
people do not have
to apologize for.
In the first centuries
of Christianity
pagans said about Christians:
"See how they love each other."
The love for God and neighbor
was the characteristic
of the first Christians.
This love was expressed
through the daily practice
of the Works of Mercy.
To feed the hungry,
to clothe the naked,

to shelter the homeless,
to instruct the ignorant
at a personal sacrifice
was considered
by the first Christians
as *the right thing to do.*
Surplus goods
were considered
to be superfluous,
and therefore
to be used
to help the needy members
of the Mystical Body.

Self-Employing Centers

The remedy for unemployment
is employment,
and there is no better employment
than self-employment.
Self-Employing Centers
are small shops
where repairs can be made
and workers can be found
to do work outside.
With the Self-Employing Centers
could be connected
Houses of Hospitality
where the self-employing workers
could find shelter.
This complicated world
is too complicated
to be dealt with
in an efficient manner
by specialized technicians.
Specialized technicians
knowing more and more
about less and less
do not know
how to simplify
a complicated world.
We need fewer specialists
and more encyclopedists,

fewer masters of one trade
and more jacks-of-all trades.

**FIVE
DEFINITIONS**

*[The following is an
analysis by Peter
Maurin of definitions
given by John
Strachey (Commu-
nist), Lawrence Den-
nis (Fascist), Norman
Thomas (Socialist)
and Stanley High
(Democrat) of their
respective beliefs.
(February, 1935)]*

What Communists Say They Believe
Communists believe
that the capitalist system
has reached the point
where it does no longer work.
Communists believe
that when the workers
come to the realization
of the downfall of capitalism
they will no longer tolerate it.
Communists believe
that the capitalist class
will resort to all means
that may be in its power
to maintain its existence.
Communists believe
that the Communist Party
knows how to assure
the production and distribution
in an orderly manner
according to a predesigned plan.

What Fascists Say They Believe
Fascists believe
in a national economy
for the protection
of national and private interests.
Fascists believe
in the regulation of industries
so as to assure
a wage for the worker
and a dividend for the investor.
Fascists believe
in class collaboration
under State supervision.
Fascists believe
in the co-operation

75

of employers' unions
and workers' unions.

What Socialists Say They Believe
Socialists believe
in a gradual realization
of a classless society.
Socialists believe
in the social ownership
of natural resources
and the means of production
and distribution.
Socialists believe
in a transition period
under democratic management
between two economic systems,
the system of production for use
and the one of production for profits.
Socialists believe
in freedom of the press,
freedom of assemblage,
freedom of worship.

What Democrats Say They Believe
Democrats believe
in universal suffrage,
universal education,
freedom of opportunity.
Democrats believe
in the right of the rich
to become richer
and of the poor
to try to become rich.
Democrats believe
in labor unions
and financial corporations.
Democrats believe
in the law of supply and demand.

What the Catholic Worker Believes
The Catholic Worker believes
in the gentle personalism

of traditional Catholicism.
The Catholic Worker believes
in the personal obligation
of looking after
the needs of our brother.
The Catholic Worker believes
in the daily practice
of the Works of Mercy.
The Catholic Worker believes
in Houses of Hospitality
for the immediate relief
of those who are in need.
The Catholic Worker believes
in the establishment
of Farming Communes
where each one works
according to his ability
and gets
according to his need.
The Catholic Worker believes
in creating a new society
within the shell of the old
with the philosophy of the new,
which is not a new philosophy
but a very old philosophy,
a philosophy so old
that it looks like new.

**WHY NOT
BE A BEGGAR?**

Share Your Wealth
What we give to the poor
for Christ's sake
is what we carry with us
when we die.
As Jean Jacques Rousseau says:
"When man dies
he carries
in his clutched hands
only that
which he has given away."

The Wisdom of Giving

To give money to the poor
is to enable the poor to buy.
To enable the poor to buy
is to improve the market.
To improve the market
is to help business.
To help business
is to reduce unemployment.
To reduce unemployment
is to reduce crime.
To reduce crime
is to reduce taxation.
So why not give to the poor
for business' sake,
for humanity's sake,
for God's sake?

IN THE LIGHT OF HISTORY

The Communist Party

The criticism of bourgeois capitalism
by the Communist Party
is the criticism
of Victor Considerant
used by Marx and Engels
in the Communist Manifesto.
The definition of Communism
of the Communist Manifesto
is the definition
of Proudhon
borrowed by Marx and Engels.
The technique of class struggle
is the technique
advocated by Marx and Engels.
The technique of proletarian dictatorship
is the technique
advocated by Lenin.

The Catholic Worker

The Catholic Worker criticism
of bourgeois society
is the criticism
of St. Thomas More.

The Catholic Worker aims
are the aims
of St. Thomas Aquinas
in his doctrine
of the Common Good.
The Catholic Worker means
are the daily practice
of the Works of Mercy
and the fostering
of Farming Communes
where scholars
become workers
and workers
become scholars.

1200—Guild System
In 1200 A. D.
there was no capitalist system,
there was the guild system.
The doctrine of the guilds
was the doctrine
of the Common Good.
People used to say, as they do now,
"What can I do for you?"
but they meant what they said.
Now they say one thing
and they mean another.
They did not look for markets,
they let the markets
look for them.

1400—Middle Men
Around 1400 A. D.
appears the middle man.
He offers to buy the goods
and to find a market.
The guildsman
thinks about the money
offered for his goods
and forgets the Common Good.
And the middle man
is not interested

in selling useful goods
but in making money
on any kind of goods.
And the consumer
never meets the producer
and the producer
ceases to think
in terms of service
and begins to think
in terms of profits.

1600—Banker
Before John Calvin
people were not allowed
to lend money at interest.
John Calvin decided
to legalize
money lending at interest
in spite of the teachings
of the Prophets of Israel
and the Fathers of the Church.
Protestant countries
tried to keep up
with John Calvin
and money-lending at interest
became the general practice.
And money ceased to be
a means of exchange
and began to be
a means to make money.
So people lent money on time
and started to think of time
in terms of money
and said to each other,
"Time is money."

1700—Manufacturer
With the discovery of steam
the factory system
made its appearance.
To take drudgery out of the home
was supposed to be

the aim of the manufacturer.
So the guildsman
left his shop
and went to the factory.
But the profit-making manufacturer
found it more profitable
to employ women
than to employ men.
So the women left the home
and went to the factory.
Soon the children
followed the women
in the factory.
So the men have to stay at home
while the women and children
work in the factory.

1800—Economist
Since Adam Smith,
who published his book in 1776,
we have been told
that competition
is the life of trade
and that it is a case
of the survival of the fittest.
So since 1776
looking for markets
has engaged men's activities.
And since trade follows the flag,
industrial nations
have also become
imperialist nations.
The fight for markets
between two industrial nations,
England and Germany,
was the main cause
of the World War.

1914—World War
As President Wilson said,
the World War
was a commercial war.

But a commercial war
had to be idealized,
so it was called
a War for Democracy.
But the War for Democracy
did not bring Democracy,
it brought
Bolshevism in Russia,
Fascism in Italy,
Nazism in Germany.

1929—World Depression
After the World War
people tried to believe
that a New Era
had dawned upon the world.
People thought
that they had found a solution
to the problem
of mass distribution.
People thought
that the time had come
of a two-car garage,
a chicken in every pot
and a sign "To Let"
in front of every poorhouse.
And everybody
wanted to cash in
on the future prosperity.
So stock promoters got busy
and stocked people with stocks
till they got stuck.

1933—New Deal
We were told in 1929
that business would go on
as usual.
We were told in 1930
that the economic system
was fundamentally sound.
We were told in 1931
that prosperity

was just around the corner.
We were told in 1932
that the depression was fought
on one hundred fronts.
We were told in 1933
that five million men
would be employed
by Labor Day.
And in 1934
people went crazy
for the NRA.
And in 1935
the NRA is scrapped
and economic recovery
is a long way off.

1933—The Catholic Worker

The aim of the Catholic Worker
is to create order
out of chaos.
The aim of the Catholic Worker
is to help the unemployed
to employ themselves.
The aim of the Catholic Worker
is to make an impression
on the depression
through expression.
The aim of the Catholic Worker
is to create a new society
within the shell of the old
with the philosophy of the new,
which is not a new philosophy,
but a very old philosophy,
a philosophy so old
that it looks like new.

TEACHERS, TRADERS, AND TRICKSTERS

No Recourse

Politicians used to say:
"We make prosperity
through our wise policies."
Business men used to say:
"We make prosperity

through our private enterprise."
The workers did not seem
to have anything to do
about the matter.
They were either
put to work
or thrown out
of employment.
And when unemployment came
the workers had no recourse
against the professed
makers of prosperity—
politicians
and business men.

Politics Is Politics
A politician is an artist in the art
of following the wind
of public opinion.
He who follows the wind
of public opinion
does not follow
his own judgment.
And he who does not follow
his own judgment
cannot lead people
out of the beaten path.
He is like the
the tail end of the dog
trying to lead the head.
When people stand back
of politicians
and politicians
stand back of the people,
people and politicians
go around in a circle
and get nowhere.

Maker of Deals

A business man
is a maker of deals.
He wants to close
a profitable deal
in the shortest possible time.
To close a profitable deal
in the shortest possible time
he tells you
what a good bargain
you are getting.
And while he tells you
what a good bargain
you are getting
he is always thinking
what a good bargain
he is getting.
He appeals
to the selfishness in you
to satisfy
the selfishness in him.

Business Is Selfishness

Because everybody
is naturally selfish
business men say
that business
must be based
on selfishness.
But when business
is based on selfishness
everybody is busy
becoming more selfish.
And when everybody is busy
becoming more selfish
we have classes and clashes.

Teaching Subjects

Our business managers
don't know how to manage
the things they try to manage
because they don't understand

the things they try to manage.
So they turn to college professors
in the hope of understanding
the things they try to manage.
But college professors
do not profess anything;
they only teach subjects.
As teachers of subjects
college professors
may enable people
to master subjects.
But mastering subjects
has never enabled anyone
to master situations.

Specialization

A few years ago,
I asked a college professor
to give me
the formulation
of those universal concepts
embodied
in the universal message
of universal universities
that will enable
the common man
to create
a universal economy.
And I was told
by the college professor:
"That is not my subject."
Colleges and universities
give to the students
plenty of facts
but very little understanding.
They turn out specialists
knowing more and more
about less and less.

Christianity Untried
Chesterton says:
"The Christian ideal
has not been tried
and found wanting.
It has been found difficult
and left untried."
Christianity has not been tried
because people thought
it was impractical.
And men have tried everything
except Christianity.
And everything
that men have tried
has failed.

St. Thomas More

St. Thomas More believed
in the Common Law.
The Common Law
that St. Thomas More
believed in
was rooted
in Canon Law.
Henry VIII believed
that since he was king
he was the Law.
St. Thomas More
did not believe
in Henry VIII's
interpretation
of Common Law.
The Common Law
as it exists
in today's England
has little relation
to Canon Law.

Judge Cardozo

Judge Cardozo said
that Common Law
as it exists today
in the United States
does not make sense.
Judge Cardozo proposed
to discard Common Law
and go back
to Roman Law.
If modern Common Law
is bad,
modern Roman Law
is worse.
"To grab and to hold"
is the aim
of Roman Law.
"Divide to rule"

is the motto
of the Roman Law-minded Lawyers.

Arthur Penty
In a book entitled:
*A Guildsman's
Interpretation of History*
Arthur Penty
has a chapter
on the revival
of Roman Law.
The revival
of Roman Law
in the 13th century
brought about the disputes
between Kings and Popes.
The Kings
are on the go.
The Pope
is still on the job.
He writes encyclicals,
but business men
and politicians
pay little attention
to what he has to say.
In the meantime,
we are worrying
about what Stalin, Hitler and Mussolini
will do to us.

Catholic Bourgeois

A bourgeois is a man
who tries to be somebody,
by trying to be like everybody,
which makes him a nobody.
Catholic bourgeois
try to be
like non-Catholic bourgeois
and think they are
just as good
as non-Catholic bourgeois.
Right after the war
Catholic bourgeois
tried to believe
what non-Catholic bourgeois
tried to believe,
that the time had come
in America
for a two-car garage
a chicken in every pot
and a sign "To Let"
in front of every poorhouse.
And Catholic colleges
as well as non-Catholic colleges
turned out stock promoters,
stock brokers
and stock salesmen
who stocked people with stocks
till they got stuck.

Shouting With Rotarians

Modern colleges
give you
a bit of this,
a bit of that,
a bit of something else
and a degree.
The act of giving a degree
is called a Commencement.
And after the Commencement
the student commences
to look for a job.

College Graduates

Sociology is not a science,
it is an art.
The art of sociology
is the art
of creating order
out of chaos.
Bourgeois colleges
turn out college graduates
into a changing world
without ever telling them
how to keep it from changing
or how to change it
so as to make it fit
for college graduates.
College graduates
think in terms of jobs,
not in terms of work.
Since the world is upside down,
taking the side down
and putting it up
should be the task
of college graduates.
But college graduates
would rather
play somebody else's game
in a position
than to create order
out of chaos.

An Unhappy Lot

But the job providers
are not on the job
and college graduates
are disappointed.
They have degrees,
but their degrees
do not give them jobs.
They have been told
that the road to success
is a college education.
They have a college education

and they do not know
what to do,
with themselves.
The overproduction
of college graduates
is a fertile ground
for social demagogues.
The unemployed college graduates
are getting sore
at their parents
for sending them into colleges
which have not prepared them
for a changing world.
And they ask themselves
if their educators
know what it is
to be educated.

Houses of Hospitality
In the *New Masses*
a Communist cartoonist represents
a line of college graduates
receiving their degrees
from the Alma Mater
and joining a soup line
on the other side of the square.
Social reconstruction
will be the result
of social indoctrination.
But unemployed college graduates
cannot be indoctrinated
without first being fed,
as well as clothed,
as well as sheltered.
Houses of Hospitality
for unemployed college graduates
are a pressing need.

Indoctrination
In Houses of Hospitality
unemployed college graduates

will be fed, clothed, sheltered,
as well as indoctrinated.
Unemployed college graduates
must be told
why the things are
what they are,
how the things would be
if they were
as they should be
and how a path
can be made
from the things
as they are
to the things
as they should be.
Unemployed college graduates
must be told
how to create
a new society
within the shell of the old
with the philosophy of the new,
which is not a new philosophy,
but a very old philosophy,
a philosophy so old
that it looks like new.

On Farming Communes

When unemployed college graduates
will have been indoctrinated
they will be moved
to Farming Communes.
On Farming Communes
unemployed college graduates
will be taught
how to build their houses,
how to gather their fuel,
how to raise their food,
how to make their furniture;
that is to say,

how to employ themselves.
Unemployed college graduates
must be taught
how to use their hands.
Unemployed college graduates
have time
on their hands.
And while time is on the hands
of college graduates
their heads don't function
as they should function.
On Farming Communes
unemployed college graduates
will learn to use
both their hands
and their heads.

SOCIAL WORKERS AND WORKERS

The training of social workers
enables them to help people
to adjust themselves
to the existing environment.
The training of social workers
does not enable them
to help people
to change the environment.
Social workers
must become social-minded
before they can be critics
of the existing environment
and free creative agents
of the new environment.
In Houses of Hospitality
social workers can acquire
that art of human contacts
and that social-mindedness
or understanding of social forces
which will make them critical
of the existing environment
and the free creative agents
of a new environment.

BOOK 3

BACK TO CHRIST—
BACK TO THE LAND!

On the Level

Owen Young says:
"We will never have prosperity
as long as there is no balance
between industry
and agriculture."
The farmer sells
in an open market
and is forced to buy
in a restricted market.
When the farmer gets
a pair of overalls
for a bushel of wheat
the wheat and the overalls
are on the level.
When the farmer
has to give
two bushels of wheat
for a pair of overalls
the wheat and the overalls
are not on the level.
Wheat and overalls
must be on the level.

Industrialization

Lenin said:
"The world cannot be
half industrial
and half agricultural."
England, Germany,
Japan and America
have become
industrialized.
Soviet Russia
is trying to keep up
with England, Germany,
Japan and America.
When all the world
will be industrialized
every country
will be looking
for foreign markets.

But when every country
will be industrialized
you will not have
foreign markets.

Mechanized Labor
Gandhi says:
"Industrialism is evil."
Industrialism is evil
because it brings idleness
both to the capitalist class
and the working class.
Idleness does no good
either to the capitalist class
or to the working class.
Creative labor
is what keeps people
out of mischief.
Creative labor
is craft labor.
Mechanized labor
is not creative labor.

No Pleasure in Their Work
Carlyle says:
"He who has found his work,
let him look
for no other blessedness."
But workmen
cannot find happiness
in mechanized work.
As Charles Devas says,
"The great majority
having to perform
some mechanized operation
which requires little thought
and allows no originality
and which concerns an object
in the transformation of which,
whether previous or subsequent,
they have no part,
cannot take pleasure

in their work."
As D. Marshall says,
"Previously the workman
fashioned every article
with his own hands,
bringing to bear on it
all the skill of the craft
which was his;
now all of this
is done by the machine."

Industrialism and Art
Eric Gill says:
"The notion of work
has been separated
from the notion of art.
The notion of the useful
has been separated
from the notion of the beautiful.
The artist,
that is to say,
the responsible workman,
has been separated
from all other workmen.
The factory hand
has no responsibility
for what he produces.
He has been reduced
to a sub-human condition
of intellectual irresponsibility.
Industrialism
has released the artist
from the necessity
of making anything useful.
Industrialism
has also released the workman
from making anything amusing."

From a Chinese
A Chinese says:
"I thought I had become Westernized
but now I am becoming repatriated.

The material progress of America
had dazzled me.
I wished while there
to transplant what I saw
to China.
But now that I am home again
I see that our two civilizations
have irreconcilable differences.
Yours is a machine civilization;
ours is a handicraft civilization.
Your people
work in factories;
our people
work in shops.
Your people
produce quantity things
that are alike;
our people
produce quality things
that are different.
What would Western industrialism
do to us?
Our people
would become robots.
Our cultural traditions
would be destroyed."

Regard for the Soil
Andrew Nelson Lytle says:
"The escape from industrialism
is not in Socialism
or in Sovietism.
The answer lies
in a return to a society
where agriculture is practiced
by most of the people.
It is in fact impossible
for any culture
to be sound and healthy
without a proper respect
and proper regard
for the soil,

no matter
how many urban dwellers
think that their food
comes from groceries
and delicatessens
or their milk from tin cans.
This ignorance
does not release them
from a final dependence
upon the farm."

Up to Catholics

Ralph Adams Cram says:
"What I propose
is that Catholics
should take up
this back-to-the-land problem
and put it into operation.
Why Catholics?
Because they realize
more clearly than any others
the shortcomings
of the old capitalist
industrial system.
They, better than others,
see the threat
that impends.
They alone understand
that while the family
is the primary social unit,
the community comes next.
And there is
no sound
and righteous
and enduring community
where all its members
are not substantially
of one mind
in matters of the spirit—
that is to say,
of religion."

INSTITUTIONS VS. CORPORATIONS

In the first issue of
The Catholic Worker
appeared this essay:

Institutions and Corporations

Jean Jacques Rousseau says:
"Man is naturally good,
but institutions make him bad,
so let us
overthrow institutions."
I say: Man is partly good
and partly bad,
but corporations,
not institutions,
make him worse.
"An institution," says Emerson,
"is the extension
of the soul of a man."
Institutions are founded
to foster the welfare
of the masses.
Corporations are organized
to promote wealth
for the few.
So let us found
smaller and better
institutions
and not promote
bigger and better
corporations.

Some Institutions

Round-Table Discussions
to learn from scholars
how the things would be
if they were
as they should be.
Campion Propaganda Committees
for the indoctrination
of the man of the street.
Maternity Guilds
for the welfare
of needy mothers
bringing young children
into the world.
Houses of Hospitality

to give to the rich
the opportunity
to serve the poor.
Farming Communes
where the scholars
may become workers
so the workers
may be scholars.

American Institutions
The American Constitution,
the American Congress,
the American Supreme Court
are also considered
as institutions.
The American Constitution
was devised
by the American Founders
to protect the individual
against the majority,
whether in Congress
or government.
The American Supreme Court
was established by the Founders
to watch over the Constitution
so as to prevent
its misrepresentation
and its misapplication.

Bureaucracy
Bureaucracy has failed,
whether in America,
in France or Germany.
In France we say:
"*Plus ça change,
plus c'est la même chose.*"
[The more it changes,
the more it remains
the same thing.]
Governments change
but the bureaucracy remains.

Political corruption
has made the French people
disgusted with their politicians.
The most efficient bureaucracy
was the German bureaucracy.
And the faith in bureaucracy
was so great
that they failed
to create a public opinion
for democratic reform.
So the Nazis beat them to it.
And created a public opinion
for racial demagogy.
The Catholic Worker
is trying to create
a public opinion
for Communitarian reform.

Five Definitions

A Bourgeois
is a fellow
who tries to be somebody
by trying to be
like everybody,
which makes him
a nobody.
A Dictator
is a fellow
who does not hesitate
to strike you over the head
if you refuse to do
what he wants you to do.
A Leader
is a fellow
who refuses to be crazy
the way everybody else is crazy
and tries to be crazy
in his own crazy way.
A Bolshevist
is a fellow
who tries to get
what the other fellow has

and to regulate
what you should have.
A Communitarian
is a fellow
who refuses to be
what the other fellow is
and tries to be
what he wants him to be.

They and We
People say:
"They don't do this,
they don't do that,
they ought to do this,
they ought to do that."
Always "They"
and never "I."
People should say:
"They are crazy
for doing this
and not doing that
but I don't need
to be crazy
the way they are crazy."
The Communitarian Revolution
is basically
a personal revolution.
It starts with I,
not with They.
One I plus one I
makes two I's
and two I's make We.
We is a community,
while "they" is a crowd.

A New Movement
The Nazis, the Fascists
and the Bolshevists
are Totalitarians.
The Catholic Worker
is Communitarian.

The principles of Communitarianism
are expounded every month
in the French magazine *Esprit* (the Spirit).
Emmanuel Mounier,
editor of the magazine,
has a book entitled
"*La Révolution Personnaliste et
Communautaire.*"

A NEW
SOCIAL ORDER

The Hope of the People

The Marxists say
that religion
is the dope of the people.
Religion is not the dope of the people,
it is the hope of the people.
Modern society
is a materialist society
because Christians have failed
to translate the spiritual
into the material.
If Christians knew
how to make a lasting impression
on the materialist depression
through spiritual expression
Marxists would not say
that religion
is the dope of the people.
As Raymond de Becker says:
"The social task of the laity
is the sanctification
of secular life,
or more exactly,
the creation
of a Christian secular life."

The Christian Front

The Christians
who consider religion
the hope of the people
should not unite
with the Marxists
who consider religion

the dope of the people.
As the editors of the *Christian Front* say:
"Marxism not only falsifies
the origin and the end of man
but it seeks to make of him
an anonymous animal,
a servant
of the proletarian State."
The editors of the *Christian Front*
are not liberals,
they think that men
"must take their choice
to stand for Christianity
or to stand for what opposes it."
They ask the Christians
"to dissociate themselves
from an un-Christian social order
and prepare the way
for a social order
compatible with their beliefs."

The New Apologetics
In his lectures
on the New Christendom
Jacques Maritain
emphasizes the necessity
of laying the foundations
of a new social order.
Laying the foundations
of a new social order
is the task of the laity.
The task of the laity
is to do the pioneer work
of creating order
out of chaos.
The clergy teach the principles;
the task of the laity
is to apply them
without involving the clergy
in the application.
The application to the social problems
by the Catholic laity

of the Catholic principles
taught by the Catholic clergy
is a new kind of apologetics,
a kind of apologetics
Catholics will not have
to apologize for.

**YES!
I AM A RADICAL**

Down to the Roots
I was once thrown out
of a Knights of Columbus meeting
because, as the K. of C. official said,
I was radical.
I was introduced as a radical
before the college students
of a Franciscan college,
And the Franciscan Father added
"I am as radical
as Peter Maurin."
Speaking in a girls' college
near St. Cloud, Minnesota,
I was told by Bishop Busch,
"Conservatives
are up in a tree
and you are trying
to go down to the roots."

Poor Conservatives
After another meeting
I was told by a sociologist
"I still think
that you are a radical."
And I told the sociologist
"We have to pity
those poor conservatives
who don't know
what to conserve;
who find themselves
living in a changing world
while they do not know
how to keep it from changing
or how to change it
to suit themselves."

Radically Wrong

Monsignor Fulton Sheen says:
"Modern society is based on greed."
Father McGowan says:
"Modern society
is based on systematic selfishness."
Professor John Dewey says:
"Modern society
is based on rugged individualism."
When conservatives
try to conserve a society
based on greed,
systematic selfishness
and rugged individualism
they try to conserve something
that is radically wrong,
for it is built
on a wrong basis.
And when conservatives
try to conserve
what is radically wrong
they are also
radically wrong.

A New Society

To be radically right
is to go to the roots
by fostering a society
based on creed,
systematic unselfishness
and gentle personalism.
To foster a society
based on creed
instead of greed,
on systematic unselfishness
instead of systematic selfishness,
on gentle personalism
instead of rugged individualism,
is to create a new society
within the shell of the old.
Modern society

is in a state of chaos.
And what is chaos
if not lack of order?
Sociology
is not a science,
it is an art,
the art of creating order
out of chaos.
All founders of orders
made it their personal business
to try to solve the problems
of their own day.
If religious orders
made it their business
to try to solve the problems
of our own day
by creating order
out of chaos,
the Catholic Church
would be the dominant
social dynamic force
in our day and age.

FEEDING THE POOR   **At a Sacrifice**
In the first centuries
of Christianity
the hungry were fed
at a personal sacrifice,
the naked were clothed
at a personal sacrifice,
the homeless were sheltered
at personal sacrifice.
And because the poor
were fed, clothed and sheltered
at a personal sacrifice,
the pagans used to say
about the Christians
"See how they love each other."
In our own day
the poor are no longer
fed, clothed and sheltered
at a personal sacrifice,

at a personal sacrifice,
but at the expense
of the taxpayers.
And because the poor
are no longer
fed, clothed and sheltered
the pagans say about the Christians
"See how they pass the buck."

RADICALS OF THE RIGHT

Shouting a Word

Father Parsons says:
"There is
confusion of mind."
When there is
confusion of mind
someone has only
to shout a word
and people flock.
When Mussolini
shouted discipline
people flocked.
When Hitler
shouted restoration
people flocked.

The Right Word

Mussolini's word is
discipline.
Hitler's word is
restoration.
My word is
tradition.
I am a radical
of the right.
I go right to the right
because I know
it is the only way
not to get left.
Sound principles
are not new,
they're very old;

they are as old
as eternity.
The thing to do
is to restate
the never new
and never old principles
in the vernacular
of the man of the street.
Then the man of the street will do
what the intellectual
has failed to do;
that is to say,
"do something about it."

Philosophy and Sophistry
Mortimer Adler says:
"Modern philosophers
have not found
anything new
since Aristotle."
Modern philosophers
are not philosophers;
they are sophists.
Aristotle
had to deal
with sophists
in his day and age.
What Aristotle said
to the sophists
of his own day
could be read
with profit
by modern philosophers.

The City of God
Jacques Maritain says:
"There is more in man
than man."
Man was created
in the image of God;
therefore

there is the image of God
in man.
There is more to life
than life
this side of the grave;
there is life
the other side of the grave.
Science leads to biology,
biology to psychology,
psychology to philosophy,
philosophy to theology.
Philosophy
is the handmaid
of theology.
To build up the City of God,
that is to say,
to express the spiritual
in the material
through the use
of pure means,
such is the task
of professing Christians
in this day and age.

Integral Humanism

Through the influence
of Maxim Gorki
the Marxists
have come to the conclusion
that Marxist writers
should be more
than proletarian writers;
that they should be
cultural writers.
Waldo Frank thinks
that the cultural tradition
must be brought
to the proletarian masses,
who will appreciate it
much more
than the acquisitive classes.
What the Marxists

call culture
Maritain calls
Socialist Humanism.
But Socialist Humanism
is not all Humanism,
according to Maritain.
In a book entitled
"L'Humanisme intégral"
Jacques Maritain points out
what differentiates
Integral Humanism
from Social Humanism.

Thought and Action
Integral Humanism
is the Humanism
of the Radicals of the Right.
The Radicals of the Left
are now talking about
Cultural Tradition.
The bourgeois idea is
that culture
is related to leisure.
Eric Gill maintains
that culture
is related to work,
not to leisure.
Man is saved through faith
and through works,
and what one does
has a lot to do
with what one is.
Thought and action
must be combined.
When thought
is separated from action,
it becomes academic.
When thought
is related to action
it becomes dynamic.

Two Bourgeois

The bourgeois capitalist
believes in rugged individualism;
The Bolshevist Socialist
believes in rugged collectivism.
There is no difference
between the rugged individualism
of bourgeois capitalism
and the rugged collectivism
of Bolshevist Socialism.
The bourgeois capitalist
tries to keep
what he has,
and tries to get
what the other fellow has.
The Bolshevist Socialist
tries to get
what the bourgeois capitalist has.
The Bolshevist Socialist
is the son
of the bourgeois capitalist,
and the son
is too much
like his father.
All the sins of the father
are found in the son.

Bourgeois Capitalist

The bourgeois capitalist
calls himself conservative
but has failed to conserve
our cultural tradition.
He thinks that culture
is related to leisure.
He does not think that culture
is related to cult
and to cultivation.
He believes in power,
and that money
is the way to power.
He believes that money
can buy everything,

whether it be labor or brains.
But as the poet Emerson says,
"People have only
the power we give them."
When people will cease
selling their labor power
or their brain power
to the bourgeois capitalist,
the bourgeois capitalist
will cease being
a gentleman of leisure
and begin being
a cultured gentleman.

Bolshevist Socialist
The Bolshevist Socialist
is the spiritual son
of the bourgeois capitalist;
he credits bourgeois capitalism
with an historic mission
and fails to condemn it
on general principles.
The bourgeois Socialist
does not believe
in the profit system,
but he does believe
in the wage system.
The bourgeois capitalist
and his spiritual son,
the Bolshevist Socialist,
believe in getting
all they can get
and not in giving
all they can give.
The bourgeois capitalist
and his spiritual son,
the Bolshevist Socialist,
are go-getters,
not go-givers.

The Personalist Communitarian
A personalist
is a go-giver,

not a go-getter.
He tries to give
what he has,
and does not
try to get
what the other fellow has.
He tries to be good
by doing good
to the other fellow.
He is altro-centered,
not self-centered.
He has a social doctrine
of the common good.
He spreads the social doctrine
of the common good
through words and deeds.
He speaks through deeds
as well as words,
for he knows that deeds
speak louder than words.
Through words and deeds
he brings into existence
a common unity,
the common unity
of a community.

Community Spirit
Communitarianism
is the rediscovery
and the exemplification
of what the Kiwanis
and Rotarians
used to talk about,
namely,
the community spirit.
The community spirit
is no more common
than common sense
is common.
Everybody knows
that common sense
is not common,

but nobody believes
that common sense
should not be common.
The community spirit
should be common.
as well as common sense
should be common.
If common sense was common,
Bolshevist Socialists
would not be
rugged collectivists;
they would be
Communitarian personalists.

Franciscans and Jesuits
Franciscans and Jesuits
believe in the community spirit
just as much
as Kiwanis and Rotarians.
While Kiwanis and Rotarians
used to talk about the common spirit,
Franciscans and Jesuits
did something about it.
Kiwanis and Rotarians
used to talk
about service
but never forgot
profitable service.
Franciscans and Jesuits
may not say much
about service,
but continue to render
unprofitable service.
Franciscans and Jesuits
believe in the responsibility
of private property
but they believe also
in the practicality
of voluntary poverty.

Counsels of the Gospel

Someone said
that *The Catholic Worker*
is taking monasticism
out of the monasteries.
The Counsels of the Gospel
are for everybody,
not only for monks.
Franciscans and Jesuits
are not monks.
Franciscans are Friars,
and the world is their monastery.
Jesuits are the storm troops
of the Catholic Church,
and ready to be sent
where the Holy Father
wishes to send them.
The Counsels of the Gospel
are for everybody,
and if everybody
tried to live up to it
we would bring order
out of chaos,
and Chesterton would not
have said
that the Christian ideal
has been left untried.

COMMUNITARIAN PERSONALISM

Basic Power

Bourgeois capitalism
is based on the power
of hiring and firing.
Fascist Corporatism
and Bolshevist Socialism
are based on the power
of life and death.
Communitarian Personalism
is based on the power
of thought and example.

Thinking Is Individual

Thinking is individual,
not collective.
Fifty million Frenchmen
may be wrong,
while one Frenchman
may be right.
One thinks
better than two,
and two
better than two hundred.
The national thinking
of Benito Mussolini,
the racial thinking
of Adolph Hitler
and the mass thinking
of Joseph Stalin
are not what I mean
by thinking.
Read *The Crowd*,
by Gustave LeBon.

Social Power

Social power
is more important
than political power.
And political power
is not the road
to social power.
The road to social power
is the right use
of liberty.
Read *Our Enemy the State*,
by Albert Jay Nock.

Give Me Liberty

Patrick Henry said,
"Give me liberty,
or give me death!"
What makes man
a man
is the right use
of liberty.

The rugged individualists
of the Liberty League,
the strong-arm men
of the Fascist State
and the rugged collectivists
of the Communist Party
have not yet learned
the right use
of liberty.
Read *Freedom in the Modern World,*
by Jacques Maritain.

Leadership

Everybody
looks for a leader
and nobody
likes to be dictated to.
Mussolini, Hitler and Stalin
try to be at the same time
leaders and dictators.
A leader is a fellow
who follows a cause
in words and deeds.
A follower is a fellow
who follows the leader
because he sponsors the cause
that the leader follows.
Read *Leadership or Domination,*
by Paul Piggors.
Paul Piggors
makes a case for domination
in times of crisis,
and in this he is wrong.
Domination is not the way
to create order
out of chaos.
Leadership is always the way
to create order
out of chaos.

Communitarian Personalism

"A man is a man

for all that,"
says Robert Burns.
To bring out
the man in man,
such is the purpose
of the Communitarian Movement.
A Communitarian is a fellow
who refuses to be
what the other fellow is,
and chooses to be
what he wants
the other fellow
to be.
Read *Easy Essays*,
by Peter Maurin.

SUPERFLUOUS GOODS

The Problem of Today

General Johnson says
that the problem of today
is not to increase
producing power,
but to increase
the consuming power.
Saving to invest
is considered
a bourgeois virtue,
while spending to consume
is considered
a bourgeois vice.
While the thrifty bourgeois
increases the producing power
the bourgeois spendthrift
increases the consuming power.

With Our Superfluous Goods

Bishop von Ketteler says
that we are bound
under pain of mortal sin
to relieve the extreme needs
of our needy brother
with our superfluous goods.
With our superfluous goods

we build white elephants
like the Empire State Building.
With our superfluous goods
we build power houses
which increase the producing power
and therefore
increase unemployment.
With our superfluous goods
we build colleges
which turn out students
into a changing world
without telling them
how to keep it from changing
or how to change it
to suit college graduates.

Ambassadors of God

What we give to the poor
for Christ's sake
is what we carry with us
when we die.
We are afraid
to pauperize the poor
because we are afraid
to be poor.
Pagan Greeks used to say
that the poor
"are the ambassadors
of the gods."
To become poor
is to become
an Ambassador of God.

We Seem to Think

St. Francis thought
that to choose to be poor
is just as good
as if one should marry
the most beautiful girl in the world.
We seem to think
that poor people
are social nuisances

and not the Ambassadors of God.
We seem to think
that Lady Poverty
is an ugly girl
and not the beautiful girl
that St. Francis of Assisi
says she is.
And because we think so,
we refuse to feed the poor
with our superfluous goods
and let the politicians
feed the poor
by going around
like pickpockets,
robbing Peter
to pay Paul,
and feeding the poor
by soaking the rich.

Dear Father:
We are living
in a period of chaos.
Our task must be
to create order
out of chaos.
Creating order
out of chaos
ought to be the task
of religious orders.
The Jesuit Order
would do well
to open up
Houses of Hospitality
for the benefit
of all college graduates,
non-Catholics
as well as Catholics.
In those Houses of Hospitality
unemployed college graduates
would be given
an historical background.
Professor Carlton Hayes says
that our religion
is the only historical religion.
A Catholic historical background
given the unemployed college graduates
in Houses of Hospitality
would be
the best antidote
to Marxist materialism.
It ought also to be
that kind of historical background
that would make them
Co-operators
or Guildists
or Distributists
or Communitarians.
It would make them
look up to the individual,
not to the State,
for the solution

of social problems.
Yours for the Green Revolution,
PETER MAURIN

**BACK
TO NEWMANISM**

President Hutchins,
of the University of Chicago, says:
"How can we call
a man educated
who has not read
any of the great books
of the Western World?
Yet today,
it is entirely possible
for a student
to graduate
from the finest
American colleges
without having read
any of them,
except perhaps Shakespeare.
Of course the student
may have read of those books,
or at least
of their authors.
But this knowledge
is gained in general
through textbooks.
And the textbooks have probably
done as much
to degrade American intelligence
as any single force."

Cardinal Newman says:
"If the intellect
is a good thing,
then its cultivation
is an excellent thing.
It must be cultivated
not only as a good thing,
but as a useful thing.
It must not be useful
in any low,

mechanical,
material sense.
It must be useful
in the spreading
of goodness.
It must be used
by the owner
for the good
of himself
and for the good
of the world."

Father Bede Jarrett says:
"The truths of a generation
become the platitudes
of the next generation."
Henrik Ibsen says:
"Thought must be rewritten
every twenty years."
That is to say
eternal principles
must at all times
be presented
in the vernacular
of the man on the street.
Emerson says
that the way
to acquire the vernacular
of the man of the street
is to go to the street
and listen
to the man of the street.
The way to become dynamic
and cease to be academic
is to rub shoulders
with the men on the street.

Some one said
that the Catholic Worker
is a movement
for down-and-outs.
And it is a movement

127

for down-and-outs,
including
down-and-out business men,
down-and-out college graduates
and down-and-out college professors.
In the Catholic Worker,
besides being fed,
clothed and sheltered,
people learn
to use their hands
as well as their heads.
And while they learn
to use their heads
to guide their hands,
the use of their hands,
improves a great deal
the working of their heads.

In Silver Springs,
a few miles
from Washington, D. C.,
the Missionaries
of the Holy Trinity
combine manual labor
with intellectual pursuits.
They go to the Catholic University
in the morning,
build their own campus
or cultivate their land
in the afternoon
and do their homework
in the evening.
While they do manual labor
their mind is taken off
their studies,
which is to the benefit
both of their health
and their studies.
In Silver Springs
scholars try to be workers
and workers
try to be scholars.

The machine
is not an improvement
on man's skill;
it is an imitation
of man's skill.
Read *Post-Industrialism*
by Arthur Penty.
The best means
are the pure means
and the pure means
are the heroic means.
Read *Freedom in the Modern World*
by Jacques Maritain.
The future of the Church
is on the land,
not in the city;
for a child
is an asset
on the land
and a liability
in the city.
Read *The Church and the Land*
by Father Vincent McNabb, O.P.

**THE THINKING
JOURNALIST**

Mark Hanna used to say:
"When a dog
bites a man,
it is not news;
but when a man
bites a dog,
it is news."
To let everybody know
that a man
has bitten a dog
is not good news;
it is bad news.

To tell everybody
that a man died
leaving two million dollars,

may be journalism,
but it is not
good journalism.
But to tell everybody
that the man died
leaving two million dollars
because he did not know
how to take them with him
by giving them to the poor
for Christ's sake
during his lifetime
is good journalism.
Good journalism
is to give the news
and the right comment
on the news.
The value of journalism
is the value of the comment
given with the news.

To be a good journalist
is to say something interesting
about interesting things
or interesting people.
The news is the occasion
for the journalist
to convey his thinking
to unthinking people.
Nothing can be done
without public opinion,
and the opinion
of thinking people
who know how
to transmit their thinking
to unthinking people.

A diary is a journal
where a thinking man
records his thinking.
The *Journal Intime*
of Frédéric Amiel
is the record of the thinking

of Frédéric Amiel.
The thinking journalist
imparts his thinking
through a newspaper
by relating his thinking
to the news of the day.
By relating his thinking
to the news of the day,
the thinking journalist
affects public opinion.

By affecting public opinion,
the thinking journalist
is a creative agent
in the making of news
that is fit to print.
The thinking journalist
is not satisfied
to be just a recorder
of modern history.
The thinking journalist
aims to be a maker
of that kind of history
that is worth recording.

THE SIT-DOWN TECHNIQUE

On Gandhi Lines
Strike news
doesn't strike me,
but the sit-down strike
is a different strike
from the ordinary strike.
In the sit-down strike
you don't strike anybody
either on the jaw
or under the belt,
you just sit down.
The sit-down strike
is essentially
a peaceful strike.
If the sit-down strike
remains a sit-down strike,
that is to say,

a strike in which you strike
by just sitting down,
it may be a means
of bringing about
desirable results.
The sit-down strike
must be conducted
on Gandhi lines,
that is to say,
according to the doctrine
of pure means
as expressed by Jacques Maritain.

In the Middle Ages
The capitalist system
is a racketeering system.
It is a racketeering system
because it is
a profiteering system.
It is a profiteering system
because it is
a profit system.
And nobody
has found the way
to keep the profit system
from becoming
a profiteering system.
Harold Laski says:
"In the Middle Ages
the idea of acquiring wealth
was limited
by a body of moral rules
imposed under the sanction
of religious authority."
But modern business men
tell the clergy:
"Mind your own business
and don't butt into our business."

Economic Economy
In the Middle Ages
they had a doctrine,

the doctrine
of the Common Good.
In the Middle Ages
they had an economy
which was economical.
Their economy
was based on the idea
that God wants us
to be our brothers' keepers.
They believed
in the right to work
for the worker.
They believed
in being fair
to the worker
as well as the consumer.
They believed
in doing their work
the best they knew how
for the service
of God and men.

Proper Property

Leon Harmel,
who was an employer,
not a labor leader,
says: "We have lost
the right concept of authority
since the Renaissance."
We have not only lost
the right concept of authority,
we have also lost
the right concept
of property.
The use of property
to acquire more property
is not the proper use
of property.
The right use of property
is to enable the worker
to do his work
more effectively.

The right use of property
is not to compel the worker,
under threat of unemployment,
to be a cog in the wheel
of mass production.

Speed-up System
Bourgeois capitalists
believe in the law
of supply and demand.
Through mass production,
bourgeois capitalists
increase the supply
and decrease the demand.
The speed-up system
and the extensive use
of improved machinery
has given us
technological unemployment.
As a Catholic worker
said to me:
"Ford speeds us up,
making us do
in one day
three times as much work
as before,
then he lays us off."
To speed up the workers
and then lay them off
is to deny the worker
the right to work.

Makers of Depressions
Business men used to say:
"We make prosperity
through our private enterprise."
According to business men,
the workers
have nothing to do
with the making of prosperity.
If the workers
have nothing to do
with the making of prosperity,

they have nothing to do
with the making
of business depressions.
The refusal of business men
to accept the responsibility
for business depressions
is what makes the workers
resort to sit-down strikes.
If business men
understood business
they would find the way
to increase the demand
for manufactured products,
instead of increasing the supply
through the speed-up system
and the extensive use
of improved machinery.

Collective Bargaining
Business men
have made
such a mess of things
without workers' co-operation
that they could do no worse
with workers' co-operation.
Because the workers
want to co-operate
with the business men
in the running of business
is the reason why
they sit down.
The sit-down strike
is for the worker
the means of bringing about
collective bargaining.
Collective bargaining
should lead
to compulsory arbitration.
Collective bargaining
and compulsory arbitration
will assure the worker
the right to work.

The Modern Mind
Organized labor,
whether it be
the A.F. of L.
or the C.I.O.,
is far from knowing
what to do
with the economic setup.
Organized labor,
as well as
organized capital,
is the product
of the modern mind.
The modern mind
is in such a fog
that it cannot see the forest
for the trees.
The modern mind
has been led astray
by the liberal mind.
The endorsement
of liberal economics
by the liberal mind
has given us
this separation
of the spiritual
from the material,
which we call
secularism.

Paul Chanson
Organized labor,
organized capital
organized politics
are essentially
secularist minded.
We need leaders
to lead us
in the making of a path
from the things as they are
to the things as they should be.
I propose the formation

of associations
of Catholic employers
as well as associations
of Catholic union men.
Employers and employees
must be indoctrinated
with the same doctrine.
What is sauce for the goose
is sauce for the gander.
Paul Chanson,
President of the Employers' Association
of the Port of Calais, France,
has written a book
expounding this doctrine,
Workers' Rights and the Guildist Order.

**THE LAW
OF HOLINESS**

"No man can serve two masters,
God and Mammon."
"Be perfect
as your Heavenly Father
is perfect."
"If you want
to be perfect
sell all you have,
give it to the poor
and follow Me."
—*New Testament.*
"These are hard words,"
says Robert Louis Stevenson,
"but the hard words
of a book
were the only reason
why the book was written."

In his encyclical
on St. Francis of Sales
the Holy Father says:
"We cannot accept the belief
that this command of Christ
concerns only
a select and privileged group,
and that all others

137

may consider themselves
pleasing to Him
if they have attained
a lesser degree
of holiness.
Quite the contrary is true,
as appears from the generality
of His words.
The law of holiness
embraces all men
and admits
of no exception."

There is a rub
between the rich
who like
to get richer
and the poor
who don't like
to get poorer.
The rich,
who like
to get richer,
turn to the Church
to save them
from the poor
who don't like
to get poorer.
But the Church
can only tell the rich
who like
to get richer,
"Woe to you rich,
who like
to get richer,
if you don't help the poor
who don't like
to get poorer."

Utilitarian Philosophers

After a century
of Protestantism,
England and Scotland
saw the coming out
of a philosophical thought
known in history
as Utilitarian Philosophy.
While Luther and Calvin
discarded the authority of the Church
the Utilitarian Philosophers
discarded the authority
of Divine Revelation.
They tried to convince themselves
and convince other people
that the Church and the Bible
were a handicap,
rather than a help,
in man's striving
towards the good life.

Futilitarian Economists

The Utilitarian Philosophers,
Hobbes, Locke, Hume,
were followed
by the Futilitarian Economists,
Adam Smith, Ricardo.
The Futilitarian Economists
thought that religion
had nothing to do
with business.
They thought that everything
would be lovely
if everybody took in
each other's washing.
They thought that everybody
should try to sell
what he has to sell
to the highest bidder.
So people started
to think of time
in terms of money,

and ended by shouting:
"Time is money!"

Fascism and Marxism
Now that economic liberalism
is dying out,
modern liberals
find themselves
on the spot.
They try to escape,
from what they consider to be
an untenable position.
In their attempt to escape
the shifting sands of liberalism,
they look for authority;
not the authority
of the teaching Church
but the authority
of the political State,
whether it be
the Marxist State
or the Fascist State.
Fascism is a stop-gap
between the dictatorship
of bourgeois capitalism
and the dictatorship
of Marxian Socialism.

Capitalism, Fascism, Communism
In an article
published in the *Christian Front*,
Charles P. Bruehl says:
"Those who fondly believe
that Fascism
will save the world
from Communism
are laboring under a fatal delusion.
The ideologies
of those two
are closely allied.
They have too much in common
and their differences

can be readily effaced.
The three, capitalism, Fascism, Communism
are three in a chain.
Imperceptibly
one passes
into the other.
All three are fundamentally
materialistic,
secularistic,
totalitarian."

THE WAY TO FIGHT COMMUNISM

Twenty and Forty
A Dutch convert
used to say:
"When one is not a Socialist
at twenty,
there is something wrong
with his heart;
but if one is a Socialist
at forty
there is something wrong
with his head."

Works of Mercy
The order of the day
in Catholic circles
is to fight Communism.
To denounce Communism
in Catholic halls
is not an efficient way
to fight Communism.
The daily practice
of the Works of Mercy
is a more efficient way
to fight Communism.
The daily practice
of the Works of Mercy
by the first Christians
made the pagans
say about the Christians
"See how they love each other."

Irish Scholars

When the Irish scholars
decided to lay the foundations
of medieval Europe,
they established:
Centers of Thought
in all the cities of Europe
as far as Constantinople,
where people
could look for thought
so they could have light.
Houses of Hospitality
where Christian charity
was exemplified.
Agricultural Centers
where they combined
(a) Cult—
that is to say Liturgy
(b) with Culture—
that is to say Literature
(c) with Cultivation—
that is to say Agriculture.

Chinese Catholics

Chinese Catholics
are showing us the way
to fight Communism.
Non-Catholic writers
are writing about
the mode of living
of the Brothers of St. John Baptist.
Chinese Communists
went to visit the Brothers
and told them
that their mode of living
is more perfect
than the mode of living
of the Communist Party.
The Brothers of St. John Baptist
try to exemplify
the Sermon on the Mount.
The Sermon on the Mount

is considered practical
by the Brothers of St. John Baptist.

Five Books
If you want to know
what industrialism
has done to man,
read *Man the Unknown*,
by Dr. Alexis Carrel.
If you want to know
how we got that way,
read *A Guildsman's Interpretation
of History*,
by Arthur Penty.
If you want to know
what it is
to be a bourgeois,
read *The Bourgeois Mind*,
by Nicholas Berdyaev.
If you want to know
what religion
has to do with culture,
read *Enquiries Into Religion and Culture*,
by Christopher Dawson.
If you want to know
what to do with freedom,
read *Freedom in the Modern World*,
by Jacques Maritain.

AGAINST CLASS WAR

The Trouble Has Been
Hilaire Belloc says
the modern proletarian
works less hours
and does far less
than his father.
He is not even
primarily in revolt
against insecurity.
The trouble has been
that the masses
of our towns

143

lived under
unbearable conditions.
The contracts
they were asked to fulfill
were not contracts
that were suitable
to the dignity of man.
There was no personal relation
between the man
who was exploited
and the man
who exploited him.
Wealth had lost
its sense of responsibility.

Twin Cities
In St. Paul
there are few strikers
and few Reds.
In Minneapolis
there are plenty of strikes
and plenty of Reds.
In St. Paul
the employers
try to play fair
with the workers
and the workers
with the employers.
In Minneapolis
the employers
choose to be
rugged individualists
and the workers
consent to be
rugged collectivists.
Rugged individualists
and rugged collectivists
are spiritually related.

Class-Consciousness
Georges Sorel thought
that violence

is the midwife
of existing societies.
When the employers
believe in violence
the workers also
believe in it.
Class-consciousness
among employers
brings class-consciousness
among the workers.
To do away
with class struggle
we must first of all
do away
with class-consciousness
among employers.
The workers are
what the employers
make them.
When employers
are moved by greed
the workers are inclined
to carry a grudge.

Paul Chanson Says:
Whether we like it or not
the economic system
is necessarily related
to the regime of appropriation
of the tools of production.
If Bourgeois Capitalism
appropriates the ownership
the worker becomes a serf.
If Bolshevik Socialism
monopolizes the ownership
the worker's condition
is not better.
He is reduced
to a state of slavery.
Only a Guildist
and Communitarian economy
will bring about

the worker's emancipation.
Paul Chanson,
who says those things,
is not a labor leader.
He is the President
of the Employers Association
of the Port of Calais
in France.

UNPOPULAR FRONT

The Unpopular Front
is a front composed of:
Humanists,
who try to be human
to man;
Theists,
who believe
that God wants us
to be our brother's keeper;
Christians,
who believe
in the Sermon on the Mount
as well as
the Ten Commandments;
Catholics,
who believe
in the Thomistic Doctrine
of the Common Good.

BOOK 4

Barbarians and Civilized

We call barbarians
people living
on the other side of the border.
We call civilized
people living
on this side of the border.
We civilized,
living on this side of the border,
are not ashamed
to arm ourselves to the teeth
so as to protect ourselves
against the barbarians
living on the other side.
And when the barbarians
born on the other side of the border
invade us,
we do not hesitate
to kill them
before we have tried
to civilize them.
So we civilized
exterminate barbarians
without civilizing them.
And we persist
in calling ourselves civilized.

German and French

After the fall
of the Roman Empire
German barbarians
invaded Gaul,
now called France.
The German barbarians
came as invaders
and were civilized
by the invaded.
The Gallo-Germans
living in Gaul,
now called France,
were Christians.
Through a Christian technique

the Gallo-Romans
made Christians
out of the German invaders.
So the German invaders
gave up their religion
as well as their language
and took up the religion
as well as the language
of the invaded.

Italians and Ethiopians
Italian soldiers
went to Ethiopia
to civilize the Ethiopians.
The Italian soldiers
still think
that invaders
can civilize the invaded.
But the Ethiopians
do not like the way
the Italian soldiers
try to civilize them.
The best way
to civilize the Ethiopians
is to prepare
Ethiopian young men
for the priesthood.
As Christopher Dawson says,
culture
has a lot to do
with religion.

Spaniards and Moors
Moors from Morocco
ruled part of Spain
for eight hundred years.
They imposed Mohammedanism
on the Spaniards
through the power of the sword.
After eight hundred years,
the Spanish Christians
decided to give the Moors

a dose of their own medicine.
So the Spanish Christians
drove the Moors out of Spain
through the power of the sword.
Before the war,
Spanish Christians
failed to make use
of the power of the word.
Spanish Christians
seem to have more faith
in the power of the sword
than the power of the word.
So had the Moors
when ruling part of Spain
for eight hundred years.

Stalinites and Trotskyites

Eugene Lyons says
that Lenin and Trotsky
accepted the idea
that the end
justifies the means.
They thought
that an idealistic end
could be reached
by bloody means.
Because they resorted
to bloody means,
Stalin resorts
to bloody means.
The State has not yet
withered away
and the Communist ideal
is still out of sight.

NO PARTY LINE

The Catholic Worker
is free-lance movement
not a partisan movement.
Some of the Bishops
agree with our policies
and some don't.
We are criticized
by many Catholics
for some of our policies
and especially
our Spanish policy.
The Communist Party
has a party line.
The Catholic Worker
has no party line.
There is no party line
in the Catholic Church.

BEYOND MARXISM

The U.S.S.R. means
the Union of Socialist
Soviet Republics.
There is no Communism
in Soviet Russia.
According to Karl Marx,
"Communism is a society
wherein one works
according to his ability
and gets
according to his needs."
Such a society is found
in Catholic monasteries
but not in Soviet Russia.
That is why Strachey
was told by Father McNabb,
an English Dominican,
"I am a Communist;
you are only an amateur."
In the beginning of Christianity
the hungry were fed,
the naked were clothed,
the homeless were sheltered,
the ignorant were instructed

at a personal sacrifice.
And the pagans
used to say
about the Christians,
"See how they love each other."
Father Arthur Ryan,
born in Tipperary,
used to call
this period of history
"Christian Communism."
But it is
a long, long way
to Tipperary.

**PRIESTS
AND POLICEMEN**

Jean Jacques Rousseau said:
"Man is naturally good."
Business men say:
"Man is naturally bad;
you can do nothing
with human nature."
If it is true,
as business men say,
that you can do nothing
with human nature,
then we need fewer priests
and more policemen.
But if God the Father
sent His own begotten Son
to redeem men,
then we need more priests
and fewer policemen.

**NON-CATHOLIC
CATHOLICS**

Apologetic Catholics
Some Catholics
like to apologize
for being Catholics.
Since Catholicism
is the truth,
it is foolish
to apologize
for being Catholics.

Since Catholicism
is the truth
then Catholics
ought to let non-Catholics
apologize
for not being Catholics.
To let non-Catholics apologize
for not being Catholics
is good apologetics.
To apologize
for being Catholics
is bad apologetics.

Led by the Nose
Non-Catholics say
that Catholics
are led by the nose
by the clergy.
Real Catholics
follow their consciences.
I must admit
that some Catholics
are led by the nose.
These Catholics
who are led by the nose
are not led by the nose
by the clergy.
They are led by the nose
by non-Catholics.
These Catholics
who allow themselves
to be led by the nose
by non-Catholics
ought to be called
non-Catholic Catholics.

A Wrong Way
Non-Catholic Catholics
tell us
that one cannot lead
a Catholic life
in a Protestant country.

The protestation
of Protestants
is not a protestation
against the Catholicism
of non-Catholic Catholics.
It is a protestation
against the lack
of Catholicism
of non-Catholic Catholics.
Non-Catholic Catholics
are giving to Protestants
a wrong view
of Catholicism.
To give to Protestants
a wrong view
of Catholicism
is not the right way
to make Catholics
out of Protestants.

Catholic Principles
Protestants
have principles
but Catholics
have more principles
than Protestants.
But principles
must be applied.
To have principles
and not to apply them
is worse
than not having any
Non-Catholic Catholics
fail to bring
Catholic principles
to Protestants
because
they do not dare
to exemplify
those Catholic principles
that Protestants
do not have.

Imitators

Non-Catholic Catholics
like to tell
their Protestant friends,
"we are just as good
as you are."
They ought to tell
their Protestant friends,
"we are just as bad
as you are."
Their Protestant friends
ought to tell
the non-Catholic Catholics,
"you are not
just as bad
as we are;
you are much worse
than we are
for you are
our imitators,
you are not yourselves."

**NOT LIBERALS
BUT RADICALS**

The Word Liberal

The word liberal
is used in Europe
in a different way
from the way
it is used
in America.
In Europe
a liberal is a man
who believes in liberty
without knowing
what to do with it.
Harold Laski
accuses liberals
of having used
their intelligence
without knowing
what to do with it.
Liberals
are too liberal

156

to be radicals.
To be a radical
is to go to the roots.
Liberals
don't go to the roots;
they only
scratch the surface.
The only way
to go to the roots
is to bring religion
into education,
into politics,
into business.
To bring religion
into the profane
is the best way
to take profanity
out of the profane.
To take profanity
out of the profane
is to bring sanity
into the profane.
Because we aim
to do just that
we like to be called
radicals.

**A LETTER
FROM PETER**

Dec. 28, 1938
Seattle, Wash.
Dear Dorothy:
I arrived in Seattle
safe and sound
except for a couple bruises
on the chin.
We were driving
back to Spokane
from the Jesuit
House of Studies.
Father Robinson,
dean of Gonzaga College,
was the driver.

I was sitting in the back
with a Jesuit scholastic.
Our conversation
was so interesting
for Father Robinson
that he forgot to stop
at a red light
and ran into the middle
of a city bus.
The head of his car
was smashed.
His nose was cut
while his glasses,
which he was wearing,
were not broken.
The Jesuit scholastic
had a cut
above the left eye.
I was hurt
by bumping my chin
against the front seat.
The schools being closed,
I was only able
to talk to the scholastics
in the House of Studies.
It was Bishop White
who phoned Father Robinson
about me being in town.
I am coming back to Spokane
the 9, 10, 11 January.
I spent Christmas in Butte
with Elias Seaman.
With a Catholic Hindu
student in the School of Mines
we went to midnight Mass
at a Croatian Church.
This Croatian pastor
is a great friend
of *The Catholic Worker*.
I am sending you
a fifty-dollar check,
to help pay the debts.

While in St. Paul
I paid fifty-two dollars
and forty cents
for a 5,569-mile trip.
That trip takes me
from St. Paul to Seattle,
then to Los Angeles,
then to Denver,
then to Omaha,
then to St. Paul.
I can stop
anywhere I want
and it is good
for 150 days.
They intend
to start a Catholic Worker group
in Minneapolis.
It is also a question
of a farming commune.
Father Le Beau
at St. Thomas College,
Father Loosen
at St. Mary's Hospital,
Sister Helen Angela
at St. Joseph's Hospital
are great boosters
of *The Catholic Worker*.
Dr. John Giesen
is actively connected
with a Mexican center.
Dr. Bauer,
a German sociologist,
is now at St. Thomas
and is eager to co-operate
with *The Catholic Worker*.
Before leaving St. Paul
I made a short trip
to Eau Claire
and La Crosse.
The pastor of Eau Claire
agrees with us:
the youth needs a cause.

A Y. M. C. A. secretary
in La Crosse
is very much in sympathy
with the idea
of an Unpopular Front
on Personalist Democracy.
I found that the reaction
to *The Catholic Worker* propaganda
is very favorable.
There was very little talk
either about Franco
or Father Coughlin.
I wish you all
a Happy New Year.
Yours in Christ the Worker,
PETER MAURIN

In New England

There are three kinds of people
in New England:
the foreigners,
the Irish
and the Yankees.
The foreigners of New England
have given up
their own traditions
to keep up
with the Irish.
The Irish of New England
have given up
their own scholarship
to keep up
with the Yankees.
The Yankees of New England
have given up
their New England conscience
to keep up
with the utilitarian, futilitarian
political economists
of the Manchester School
of political economy.
So what can you expect
from New England?

In Louisana

Waldo Frank says
that America
is a lost continent
and that to rediscover itself
America must go back
to Mediterranean thought.
Mediterranean thought
was brought to Louisiana
by the founders of Louisiana,
but the people of Louisiana
have turned over
the State of Louisiana
to greedy corporations.
The Catholic people

161

of the State of Louisiana
had to have
a Baptist lawyer
by the name of Huey Long
to save them
from the grip
that greedy corporations
had on the Catholic people
of the State of Louisiana.

In Texas
Spanish Franciscans
went to Texas
when Texas was part
of Old Mexico.
Spanish Franciscans
taught the Indians
to build churches,
to build schools,
to build mission-storehouses.
The ruins of those churches,
the ruins of those schools,
the ruins of those mission-storehouses
can still be seen
in the State of Texas.
But the Catholic people
of Texas
are not interested
in the ideology
of the Spanish Franciscans.
They are interested
in keeping up
with the Yankees.

In California
The Yankees were not able
to make wage-slaves
out of the Indians.
The Yankees used to say:
"A good Indian
is a dead Indian."
By combining cult,

that is to say liturgy,
with culture,
that is to say literature,
with cultivation,
that is to say agriculture,
the Spanish Franciscans
who went to California

succeeded in making willing workers
out of the Indians.
The Catholics of California
have not found the way
to do for the Catholic unemployed
what the Spanish Franciscans
did for the Indians.
In the meantime
the people of California
are looking for a panacea
at the expense
of the taxpayers.

Going to the Right
Frey of the A. F. of L.
says that the Communist Party
is pushing Roosevelt
to the left.
The A. F. of L.
does not know enough
to push Roosevelt
to the right.
Going to the left
is going towards
the Industrial Socialism
of Stalin.
Going to the right
is going towards
the Rural Communism
of the Franciscan Founders
who founded Rural Communes
in what are now
the State of Texas,
the State of New Mexico,
the State of California.

TURNING TO THE CHURCH

When I was in St. Louis
I met a Maryknoll Father
who had recently returned
to the United States
after eight years in China
as a Maryknoll Missionary.
He is pleased to see
that non-Catholics
in the United States
are much more curious
about the Catholic Church
than they were
before he left for China
ten years ago.
While modern nations
give the sad spectacle
of going back on their word,
intelligent people
are turning to the Church
as the one moral security
left in the world.
Father McSorley,
great friend of
The Catholic Worker,
has always favored
the opening of small offices
where non-Catholics
curious about the Church
could receive information.

PROSTITUTION

Prostitution of Marriage
Birth control
is not self-control.
What is not self-control
is self-indulgence.
What is self-indulgence
is prostitution of functions.
Prostitution in marriage
is prostitution of marriage.
Prostitution of marriage
is prostitution plus hypocrisy.

Prostitution of Education

To educate
is to elevate.
To elevate
is to raise.
To raise wheat
on a piece of land
is to enable
that piece of land
to produce wheat
instead of weeds.
To raise men
from the animal state
to the cultural state
is to educate men.
The teaching of facts
without understanding
is a prostitution
of education.

Prostitution of the Press

Modern newspapermen
try to give people
what they want.
Newspapermen
ought to give people
what they need.
To give people
what they want
but should not have
is to pander.
To give people
what they need,
or in other terms,
to make them want
what they ought to want,
is to foster.
To pander
to the bad in men
is to make men
inhuman to men.
To foster the good in men

is to make men
human to men.

Prostitution of Politics
The Republicans say:
"Let's turn the rascals out."
The Democrats say:
"Let's turn the rascals out."
The Republicans
call the Democrats
rascals.
The Democrats
call the Republicans
rascals.
For the Republicans
as well as
for the Democrats
politics
is just profitable business.
By making a business
out of politics
politicians
have prostituted
the noble calling
of politics.

Prostitution of Property
All the land
belongs to God.
God wants us
to be our brother's keeper.
Our superfluous goods
must be used
to relieve the needs
of our brother.
What we do for our brother
for Christ's sake
is what we carry with us
when we die.
This is what the poor are for,
to give to the rich
the occasion to do good

for Christ's sake.
To use property
to acquire more property
is not the proper use
of property.
It is a prostitution
of property.

Prostitution of the Theatre
What applies to the Press
applies also
to the Theatre.
In the Middle Ages
the Theatre
was considered
as an efficient way
of preaching.
They liked to produce
Mystery Plays.
They aimed to preach
and not to pander.
Pandering to the crowd
has brought the degradation
of the theatre.
The Theatre started
in the Church.
The Theatre has ended
in the gutter.

Prostitution of Art
In the Middle Ages
the artists
were not called artists,
they were called artisans.
When the artists
were artisans
they had the community spirit.
They had the community spirit
because they believed
in the doctrine
of the Common Good.
Now that the artists

do no longer believe
in the doctrine
of the Common Good
they sell their work
to art speculators.
As Eric Gill says,
"they have become
the lap-dogs
of the bourgeoisie."

THE ROAD TO COMMUNISM

Paraguay Reductions
In a book entitled
The Magic Mountain
Thomas Mann has a character
who has become a Jesuit
after having been a Marxist.
As a Jesuit
he could understand Communism
much better
than he could understand it
as a Marxist.
In Paraguay
the Jesuits established
a Communist society.
Part of the land
was held individually.
The other part,
known as God's land,
was cultivated in common.
The produce was used
for the maintenance
of the aged,
the infirm
and the young.

Proudhon and Marx
"Communism is a society
where each one works
according to his ability
and gets
according to his needs."
Such a definition

does not come from Marx;
it comes from Proudhon.
Proudhon wrote two volumes
on *The Philosophy of Poverty*
which Karl Marx
read in two days.
Karl Marx wrote a volume
on *The Poverty of Philosophy*.
Karl Marx
was too much of a materialist
to understand the philosophical
and therefore social value
of voluntary poverty.

THE SIXTH COLUMN   We Catholics believe
what Dualist Humanists believe,
that there is
good and bad
in men
and that men
ought to express the good
to get rid of the bad.
We Catholics believe
what Orthodox Jews
and Quakers believe:
the Fatherhood of God
and the Brotherhood of Men.
We Catholics believe
what Fundamentalists believe:
Virgin Birth
and Redemption through Christ.
We Catholics believe
what the other believers believe
plus beliefs
that the other believers
don't believe:
Papal Supremacy
and the Universal Church.

The Catholic Worker
stands for co-operativism
against capitalism.

The Catholic Worker
stands for personalism
against Socialism.
The Catholic Worker
stands for leadership
against dictatorship.
The Catholic Worker
stands for agrarianism
against industrialism.
The Catholic Worker
stands for decentralism
against totalitarianism.

ON SPECIALIZATION

Ten years ago
I asked a college professor
to give me the formulation
of those universal concepts
embodied
in the universal message
of universal universities
that would enable
the common man
to create
a universal economy.
And the college professor answered:
"That is not my subject."
College professors
are specialists
who know more and more
about less and less
and if they keep on specializing
they will end
by knowing everything
about nothing.

A Negro student
had a father
who was a Baptist minister.
The Baptist minister
gave to his son
Baptist theology

but no science.
And the son
wanted to know science.
In the University of Pittsburgh
the Negro student
learned several sciences
without correlation.
And the Negro student
was complaining
about the University of Pittsburgh
for having failed
to give him
a correlated knowledge.

Henry Adams
went to four American universities
without acquiring
a correlated knowledge.
He went to England
and failed.
He went to France
and failed.
But in France,
looking at
the Cathedral of Chartres
and the Mont Saint Michel,
he realized
that one could have acquired
a correlated knowledge
in thirteenth century France.
And he wrote a book entitled
Mont Saint Michel
and Chartres,
now published
by the American Society of Architects.

PIE IN THE SKY   Bourgeois capitalists
don't want their pie
in the sky
when they die.
They want their pie
here and now.
To get their pie
here and now
bourgeois capitalists
give us
better and bigger
commercial wars
for the sake of markets
and raw materials.
But as Sherman says,
"War is hell."
So we get hell
here and now
because bourgeois capitalists
don't want their pie
in the sky
when they die,
but want their pie
here and now.

Bolshevist Socialists,
like bourgeois capitalists,
don't want their pie
in the sky
when they die.
They want their pie
here and now.
To get their pie
here and now,
Bolshevist Socialists
give us
better and bigger
class wars
for the sake
of capturing the control
of the means of production
and distribution.

But war is hell,
whether it is
a commercial war
or a class war.
So we get hell
here and now
because Bolshevist Socialists
don't want their pie
in the sky
when they die,
but want their pie
here and now.

Bolshevist Socialists
as well as
bourgeois capitalists
give us hell
here and now
without
leaving us the hope
of getting our pie
in the sky
when we die.
We just
get hell.
Catholic Communionism
leaves us the hope
of getting our pie
in the sky
when we die
without
giving us hell
here and now.

BOOK 5

LET'S KEEP THE JEWS FOR CHRIST'S SAKE

A Mystery

The Jews
are a mystery
to themselves.
They are not a nation,
although the Zionists
try to build up one
in Palestine.
They are not a race,
for they have intermarried
with many other races.
They are not a religion,
since their belief
calls for one Temple
and the Jewish Temple
has not been in existence
for nearly 2,000 years.

In Spain

St. Vincent Ferrer,
a Spanish Dominican,
succeeded in converting
25,000 Jews.
When the Spaniards decided
to drive the Moors out
they also decided
to drive the Jews out.
St. Vincent Ferrer
tried to convert the Jews;
he did not start a crusade
to drive them out.
Driven out of Spain,
the Jews found a refuge
in Salonika,
which was then
under the Turkish flag.
Spanish is still spoken
by Jewish workmen
in Salonika.

In the Papal States

The Popes never did
start a crusade

to drive the Jews
out of the Papal States.
Jews have lived in Rome
and the adjoining territory
since the Roman Empire.
The Roman Empire
protected the Jews
living under its rule,
and so did the Popes
in the Papal States.
The Jews themselves
admit the fairness
with which they were treated
in the Papal States.

In the Shadow of the Cross
While the Spaniards
refused to keep the Jews
the Popes consented
to keep the Jews.
The Jews
were the chosen people
and they are still,
for God does not change.
Because the Jews
did not recognize Christ
is not a good reason
for acting towards them
in a non-Christian manner.
The presence of the Jews
all over the world
is a reminder to the world
of the coming of Christ.
The Jews who refused
to accept the Cross
find their best protection
in the shadow
of the Cross.

In Germany
Under the shadow of the Cross
the Jews were protected;
under the Swastika

they are persecuted.
The Cross
stands for one thing,
the Swastika
for another thing.
The Cross stands
for race equality;
the Swastika stands
for race superiority.
The Catholic Church
stands for human brotherhood,
the Nazi regime
stands for the expansion
of one race
at the expense
of the other races.

In America

The English Puritans
found a refuge
in America.
The French Huguenots
found a refuge
in America.
The Irish Catholics
found a refuge
in America.
The German Liberals
found a refuge
in America.
America
is big enough
to find a refuge
for persecuted Jews
as well as
persecuted Christians.

In Palestine

America can produce
more than it can consume.
What America needs
is more consumers.
More Jews in America

means more consumers
for America.
It is said that the Jews
flock to the cities
and become middle men,
and that there are
too many middle men
in America.
But in Palestine
the Jews are building
both cities and country.
What the Jews are doing
in Palestine
they can do also
in America.

LOGICAL AND PRACTICAL

What is not logical
is not practical,
even if it is practiced.
What is logical
is practical
even if it is not practiced.
To practice
what is not logical
though it is practical
is to be a bourgeois.
A bourgeois is a fellow
who tries to be somebody
by trying to be
like everybody,
which makes him
nobody.
To practice
what is logical
even if it is not practiced
is to be a leader.
A leader is a fellow
who follows a cause.
The Sermon on the Mount
will be called practical
when Christians make up their mind
to practice it.

The Age of Reason

In the seventeenth century
a Frenchman
by the name of Descartes
discarded Thomistic philosophy
and formulated
a philosophy of his own.
St. Thomas' philosophy
starts with Aristotle
and helps the reason
to accept revelation.
For St. Thomas Aquinas
reason is the handmaid of faith;
not so for Descartes.
The eighteenth century
became known
as the age of enlightenment
or the age of reason.
An American
by the name of Thomas Paine
wrote a book entitled
The Age of Reason.

The Age of Treason

The use of reason
was discarded
by the intellectuals
of the nineteenth century.
Romanticism,
positivism,
pragmatism,
one after another,
became the fashion
in the nineteenth century.
In a book entitled
The Treason of the Intellectuals
Julien Benda,
a French Jew,
says the intellectuals
gave up the search for truth
and consented to become

181

the paid propagandists
of nationalists
as well as capitalists.
So the age of reason
of the eighteenth century
was followed
by the age of treason
of the nineteenth century.

The Age of Chaos
And we are now
in the age of chaos.
In an age of chaos
people look
for a new order.
Because people are becoming aware
of this lack of order
they would like to be able
to create order
out of chaos.
The time
to create order
out of chaos
is now.
The germ of the present
was in the past
and the germ of the future
is in the present.
The thing to do
is to give up old tricks
and start to play new tricks.

The Age of Order
If we make
the right decisions
in the age of chaos
the effect of those decisions
will be a better order.
The new order
brought about
by right decisions

will be functional,
not acquisitive;
personalist,
not socialist;
communitarian,
not collectivist;
organismic,
not mechanistic.
The thing to do right now
is to create a new society
within the shell of the old
with the philosophy of the new,
which is not a new philosophy
but a very old philosophy,
a philosophy so old
that it looks like new.

TRUE STORIES
When I was in Spokane
a Catholic Sister
told me:
"I have a little story
to tell you
and I think
you will like it.
I met an Indian woman
who was carrying
what looked like
a white boy.
I said to her:
'You don't mean to tell me
that you married
a white man.'
'Oh no,' she said,
'Just a Frenchman'."

An Englishman
and an American
were flying over
the Egyptian Soudan.
Under them
was a stretch of houses
four miles long.

The American
asked the Englishman:
"What is the population
of this town?"
"Nine Englishmen,"
answered the Englishman.

A German
owned a fruit farm
in British Columbia.
He and his wife
were considered
as second-class citizens
by the British element.
His wife succeeded
in inducing him
to sell the fruit farm
and go back to Germany.
She could not stand
to be considered inferior
by the British element.
The English think
that they are superior
to the Germans
and the Germans think
they are superior
to the English.
They cannot stand
to be considered
inferiors.
They can give it
but cannot take it.

LET'S BE FAIR
TO THE NEGROES
FOR CHRIST'S SAKE

The anthropologists say
that the western world
is anthropologically divided
into four kinds of people,
They are:
a) the Nordics,
b) the Alpines,
c) the Mediterraneans,
d) the Negroes.

Anthropologists add
that there is nothing
in science
to prove
that one race
is superior
to another race.
Science cannot prove
that the Nordics
are superior
to another race.

Theologians say
that Christ died
for the redemption
of the Negroes
as well as
the Nordics.
The Nordics
were created
by the same Creator
and redeemed
by the same Redeemer
as the Negroes.
The redeemed Nordics
will enjoy
the beatific vision
in the same Heaven
as the Negroes.
The redeemed Nordics
receive the same Christ
at the altar rail
as the Negroes.
The redeemed Nordics
belong to the same
Mystical Body
as the Negroes.

The Holy Father
has recently selected
African Negro priests
and made them Bishops.
The Negro Bishops
of Africa
have the same powers
as the Nordic Bishops
of Germany.
Nordic Bishops
are all right
for Nordic people
and Negro Bishops
are all right
for Negro people.
The Catholic Church

wants Nordic Bishops
to lead Nordic people
and Negro Bishops
to lead Negro people.
The Catholic Church
does not differentiate
between Nordic Bishops
and Negro Bishops.

**THE STUFF
AND THE PUSH**

I was in a cafeteria
in Greenwich Village.
Two young fellows
were talking.
One said to the other,
"Your father has the stuff,
but he hasn't the push."
And the other said:
"And I have the push,
but not the stuff."
The father had the stuff,
but he could not push it,
and the son had the push,
but he had nothing to push.
Catholic journalists
have the stuff,
but do not have the push,
and non-Catholic journalists
have the push,
but do not have the stuff.

**ON AMERICAN
TRAITS**

"I have lived
in all the major dictatorships—
Russia, Italy, Germany.
My experience teaches me
that democracy
with all its faults
is better
than any of these.
My experience teaches me
that the maintenance

of personal freedom
should be
the primary consideration
of every human being.
It is never a choice
between freedom
and a full stomach.
No dictatorship
has given either."
LOUIS FISHER

At the base
of the American spirit
is the functionalism
of frontier life,
not the acquisitivism
of the Chamber of Commerce.
The American spirit
is characterized
by the love of freedom,
the spirit of initiative
and the will to co-operate.
The American
does not like
to be pushed about
and to be sent
where he does not want
to go.
Even the business man
likes to talk about
the spirit of initiative,
which he calls
free enterprise.
When in America
some one is busy
doing something
for the Common Good
he finds people
willing to co-operate.

Freedom is a duty
more than a right.

Man has a duty
to be intelligent.
Man has a duty
to choose intelligently
between two alternatives.
Man has a duty
to act intelligently,
using pure means
to reach pure aims.
To use impure means
to reach pure aims
is to take the wrong road.
You cannot go
where you want to go
by taking a road
which does not lead you there.
Having pure aims
and using pure means
is making the right use
of freedom.

The spirit of initiative
is what business men call
free enterprise.
A private enterprise
must be carried out
for the common good.
If a private enterprise
is not carried out
for the Common Good
it turns out to be
a public nuisance.
A public nuisance
produces grievances.
Personal grievances
against public nuisances
produces demagogues
who promise to wipe out
public nuisances.
The spirit of initiative
of social-minded people
brings into existence

social institutions
that make for the welfare
of the common people.

When someone
has something
considered by the common man
to be beneficial
to the Common Good
he is admired
by the common man.
The admiration
of unselfish men
who are not afraid
to take the initiative
creates a desire
among the admirers
to climb on the bandwagon
of men of initiative.
They want to be part
of an unselfish movement.
They are willing
to make sacrifices
for the common cause.
So the will to co-operate
is the result
of the daring
of unselfish men
who are not afraid
to take the initiative.

**CHRISTIANITY
AND DEMOCRACY**

The Common Good
is not common,
because common sense
does not prevail.
In a good autocracy
the Common Good
is incarnated
in a good autocrat.
In a good aristocracy
the Common Good
is incarnated
in the good aristocrats.

In a good democracy
the Common Good
is incarnated
in the good democrats.
The good democrats
are democrats
with the democratic spirit.
They are the elite
in a democracy.

Jules Beranger
followed Jusserand
as French Ambassador
in Washington.
Béranger was an agnostic
who could not conceive
of a democracy
without a cultural elite.
The elite in a democracy
is imbued
with what we call
the right spirit.
The democratic elite
is the spearhead
of a democratic society.
The democratic elite
is recruited
from all classes
of a democratic society.
The democratic elite
is not moved
by greed for wealth
or greed for power.
It is moved
by clear thinking.

Agnostic intellectuals
lack faith
in Christ the Redeemer
as well as
in God the Omnipotent.
And now

they are losing faith
in the power of man
to pull himself up
by his own bootstraps.
Faith in Christ the Redeemer,
hope in the life to come,
and charity toward all men
are motivating forces
in the fostering
of a democratic elite—
without which
a democratic society
becomes the laughing-stock
of totalitarian societies.

What a fine place
this world would be
if Dualist Humanists
tried to be human
to men.
What a fine place
this world would be
if Personalist Theists
tried to be
their brother's keeper
as God
wants them to be.
What a fine place
this world would be
if Fundamentalist Protestants
tried to exemplify
the Sermon on the Mount.
What a fine place
this world would be
if Roman Catholics
tried to keep up
with St. Francis of Assisi.

BOOK 6

ON PERSONALISM

A stone
is not an individual.
You can make little ones
out of big ones.
A tree
is an individual.
It comes
from a germ.
"Only God
can make a tree,"
says the poet.
A horse
is an individual.
The horse is not
an individual
the way the tree
is an individual.
It has animal life.
Man is an individual
and has animal life
like the horse.
Man has also reason,
which the horse has not.

As an animal,
man is an individual.
As a reasoning animal,
man is a person.
The difference
between an individual
and a person
is the power of reasoning.
Through the use of reason
man becomes aware
of the existence of God.
Through the use of reason
man becomes aware
of his rights
as well as
his responsibilities.
Man's rights and responsibilities
come from God,

who made him
a reasoning animal.
Man's primary duty
is to act
according to reason.

To guide himself
man has
not only reason
but also faith.
Faith
is not opposed to reason,
it is above reason.
The use of reason
leads to faith,
but reason
cannot understand
all the faith.
The truths of faith
that reason
cannot understand,
we call
the mysteries of faith.
To use reason
is to philosophize
and philosophy
is the handmaid of faith.
Some truths
we get through reason
and some truths
we get through faith.

Emmanuel Mounier
wrote a book entitled
A Personalist Manifesto.
Emmanuel Mounier
has been influenced
by Charles Péguy.
Charles Péguy once said:
"There are two things
in the world:
politics and mysticism."

For Charles Péguy
as well as Mounier,
politics is the struggle for power
while mysticism
is the realism
of the spirit.
For the man-of-the-street
politics
is just politics
and mysticism
is the right spirit.
In his *Personalist Manifesto*
Mounier tries to explain
what the man-of-the-street
call "the right spirit."

FIVE FORMS OF CAPITALISM

Mercantile Capitalism

In the Middle Ages
the consumer
went to the producer
and asked the producer
to produce something
for him.
There was no middle man
between the producer
and the consumer.
When the producer
started to sell his products
to the middle man
he no longer
saw the consumer.
The producer
saw only the middle man
and the consumer
saw only the middle man
and the middle man
was only interested
in buying cheap
and selling dear.
And the functional society
ceased to exist
and the acquisitive society

came into existence.
And everybody shouted:
"Time is money!"

Factory Capitalism
When the use of steam
was discovered
the middle men
started factories.
The craftsmen
deserted their craft shops
and went to work
in the factories
and became
factory hands.
Factory owners
turned out gadgets
to take drudgery
out of the home.
And then they took women
out of the home
and brought them
into factories.
And then they took children
out of the home
and brought them
into factories.
And men had to stay home
to look after young children.

Monopoly Capitalism
With the American Civil War,
monopoly capitalism
came into existence.
With monopoly capitalism
came the trusts.
With monopoly capitalism
came high tariffs
for the protection
of infant industries.
With monopoly capitalism
came unionism

for the protection
of proletarianized workers.
With monopoly capitalism
came trust-busting laws
for the protection
of the buying public.
With monopoly capitalism
came Federal laws
for the conservation
of raw materials.

Finance Capitalism
With the first World War
finance capitalism
came into existence.
With finance capitalism
came installment buying.
In January, 1927,
the *Yale Review*
published an article
by a business man
in which he said
that installment buying
has the result
of booming boom years
and starving lean years.
Installment buying
gave us the New Era
and the promise
of a two-car garage,
a chicken in every pot
and a sign "To Let"
in front of every poorhouse.
But this promise
failed to materialize
and people found themselves
in the midst of the depression.

State Capitalism
Finance capitalism
has not been able
to employ

the unemployed.
The State
has now assumed the task
of employing the unemployed.
Economic activities
are now supervised
by State bureaucrats.
State bureaucrats
can give the people
State supervision.
State supervision
is not a substitute
for personal vision.
And without personal vision
people perish.
Personalist vision
leads to personalist action.
Personalist action
means personal responsibility.
Personal responsibility
means dynamic democracy.

**EDUCATIONAL
SECULARISM**

Puritans came to America
so they could worship God
the way they wanted
to worship God.
Quakers came to America
so they could worship God
the way they wanted
to worship God.
Huguenots came to America
so they could worship God
the way they wanted
to worship God.
English Catholics
came to America
so they could worship God
the way they wanted
to worship God.

The founders of America
agreed in this,

that there is a God
and that God wants
to be worshipped.
The founders of America
did not agree
about the way
God wants
to be worshipped.
That there is a God
and that God wants
to be worshipped
is no longer taught
in the public schools
of America.
Religion
is no longer taught
in the public schools
of America,
but politics and business
are still taught
in the public schools
of America.

When religion
has nothing to do
with education,
education is only
information:
plenty of facts
but no understanding.
When religion
has nothing to do
with politics,
politics is only
factionalism:
let's turn the rascals out
so our good friends
can get in.
When religion
has nothing to do
with business
business is only

commercialism:
let's get all we can
while the getting is good.

The Marxists
and the Chambers of Commerce
agree in this,
that religion
ought to be kept
out of the public schools.
And American Protestants
keep silent
about the secularism
of the public schools.
In the nineteenth century
public schools
were the hotbeds
of bourgeois capitalism.
In the twentieth century
public schools
are the hotbeds
of Bolshevist Socialism.

IRISH CULTURE   After the fall
of the Roman Empire.
the scholars,
scattered all over
the Roman Empire,
looked for a refuge
and found a refuge
in Ireland,
where the Roman Empire
did not reach
and where the Teutonic barbarians
did not go.
In Ireland,
the scholars formulated
an intellectual synthesis
and a technique of action.
Having formulated
that intellectual synthesis

204

and that technique of action,
the scholars decided to lay
the foundations of medieval Europe.

In order to lay the foundations
of medieval Europe,
the Irish Scholars
established *Salons de Culture*
in all the cities of Europe,
as far as Constantinople,
where people could look for thought
so they could have light.
And it was
in the so-called Dark Ages
which were not so dark,
when the Irish
were the light.
But we are now living
in a real Dark Age,
and one of the reasons why
the modern age
is so dark,
is because
too few Irish
have the light.

The Irish Scholars established
free guest houses
all over Europe
to exemplify
Christian charity.
This made
pagan Teutonic rulers
tell pagan Teutonic people:
"The Irish are good people
busy doing good."
And when the Irish
were good people
busy doing good,
they did not bother
about empires.
That is why we never heard

about an Irish Empire.
We heard about
all kinds of empires,
including the British Empire,
but never about
an Irish Empire,
because the Irish
did not bother about empires
when they were busy
doing good.

The Irish Scholars established
agricultural centers
all over Europe
where they combined
cult—
that is to say liturgy
with culture—
that is to say literature,
with cultivation—
that is to say agriculture.
And the word America
was for the first time
printed on a map
in a town in east France
called Saint-Die
where an Irish scholar
by the name Deodad
founded an agricultural center.
What was done
by Irish missionaries
after the fall
of the Roman Empire
can be done today
during and after the fall
of modern empires.

CATHOLIC ACTION   **Our Business**
Catholic Bourgeois
used to tell the clergy
"Mind your own business
and don't butt in
on our business."
Catholic bourgeois
by keeping up
with non-Catholic bourgeois
have made a mess
of their own business.
And now the Holy Father
tells Catholic bourgeois
"The Bishop's business
is your business."

The Bishop's Voice

The Bishop's business
is to teach
the Christian Doctrine.
The Holy Father
appoints a Bishop
to a seat (a cathedral)
so people may hear the truth.
that will set them free.
Clergy, teachers, journalists
are the amplifiers
of the Bishop's voice.
Fathers and mothers
must also be
the Bishop's voice.
Bishop O'Hara
is fostering the teaching
of Christian Doctrine
by fathers and mothers.
Everything connected
with the teaching
of Christian Doctrine
can be called
Catholic Action No. 1.

Works of Mercy

But the Bishop,
although he is a Bishop,
cannot teach
an empty stomach.
Some people
are Bishop-shy
because they are hungry,
shivering or sleepy.
So the Bishop
asks the faithful
to feed the hungry,
clothe the naked,
shelter the homeless
at a sacrifice.
Feeding the hungry,
clothing the naked,

sheltering the homeless
at a sacrifice
was the daily practice
of the first Christians.
The daily practice
of the Works of Mercy
is what we can call
Catholic Action No. 2.

Social Reconstruction
We are asked
by the Holy Father
to reconstruct
the social order.
Reconstructing the social order
means the creation
of a Catholic society
within the shell
of a non-Catholic society
with the philosophy
of a Catholic society.
Catholic bourgeois
made the mistake
of trying to keep up
with non-Catholic bourgeois.
Catholic reconstructors
must create
a Catholic technique
in harmony
with Catholic thought.
Social reconstruction
by Catholic laymen and women
is what we can call
Catholic Action No. 3.

Three Kinds
Catholic Action No. 1,
or the teaching
of Christian Doctrine,
must be carried out
with the Bishop's supervision.
Catholic Action No. 2,
or the daily practice

of the Works of Mercy,
can be carried out
with or without
the Bishop's supervision.
Catholic Action No. 3,
or the reconstruction
of the social order,
through the foundation
of new Catholic institutions,
must be left
to the initiative
of Catholic men and women.
The function of the Bishops
is to be
not directors
but moderators.
Political action
is not to be considered
as Catholic Action.

FOR GOD'S SAKE

Honest to God

One of the slogans
of the Middle Ages
was "Honest to God."
We have ceased to be
"Honest to God."
We think more
about ourselves
than we do
about God.
We have ceased to be
God-centered
and have become
self-centered.

Father Denifle

Father Denifle
was an Austrian Dominican.
In 1872,
he delivered four sermons
in Graz, Austria,
about "Humanity,
its destiny

and the means
to achieve it."
Translated by a priest
of Covington, Kentucky,
these four sermons
were published in America
by Pustet, the editor.
Father Denifle emphasizes
that having forgotten God,
humanity
cannot realize
its own destiny.
God has not
forgotten man,
but man has
forgotten God.

American Founders
The founders of America
came to America
to serve God
the way they thought
God wants to be served.
How God
wants to be served
is no longer taught
in American schools.
How to be successful
is still taught
in American schools.
Thinking of time
in terms of money
is at the base
of the thinking
of our business men.
We put on our coins:
"In God we trust,"
but persist in thinking
that everybody else
ought to pay cash.

Cardinal Gasquet
Cardinal Gasquet

was an English Benedictine.
He was a student
of that period
of English history
that preceded
the Reformation.
In a book entitled:
The Eve of the Reformation
he points out
that externalism
—another word
for materialism—
prevailed in that period
of English history.
The externalism
of English Bishops
made them
follow the King
instead of the Pope
when the King ceased
to mind the Pope.

St. Augustine
St. Augustine said,
"Love God
and do what you please."
We do what we please
but we don't love God.
We don't love God
because we don't know God.
We don't know God
because we don't try
to know God.
And man was created
in the image of God
and every creature
speaks to us
about God
and the Son of God
came to earth
to tell us
about God.

THE PEACEABLE KINGDOM · ISAIAH 11: 6-8

INDUSTRIALISM

It Started With England

Lenin said:
"The world cannot be
half industrial
and half agricultural."
Lenin made the mistake
of industrializing Russia.
Lenin industrialized Russia
because the Japanese
industrialized Japan.
The Japanese industrialized Japan
because the Americans
industrialized America.
The Americans industrialized America
because the Germans
industrialized Germany.
The Germans industrialized Germany
because the English
industrialized England.
It started with England.

A Few Englishmen

R. H. Tawney said
that the Englishmen wear blinkers.
Because they wear blinkers
the Englishmen
lack vision.
Because they lack vision
the Englishmen
are very strong
for supervision.
And supervision
is not a substitute
for vision.
A few Englishmen
got rid of their blinkers.
Among the Englishmen
who got rid of their blinkers
one can name:
William Cobbett,
John Ruskin,
William Morris,

Arthur Penty,
Hilaire Belloc,
G. K. Chesterton,
Eric Gill.
The best of all
is Eric Gill.

Legalized Usury
"The sex problem,
the marriage problem,
the crime problem,
the problem of armaments
and international trade,
all those problems
could be solved
if we would recognize
the necessity
of abolishing
trade in money,
and especially
the international trade in money;
that is to say,
the usury,
the legalized usury,
practiced by the banks
under the protection
of their charters
with the support
of the so-called
orthodox economists.
That is the first thing
to be recognized."

God and Mammon
Christ says:
"The dollar you have
is the dollar you give
to the poor
for My sake."
The banker says:
"The dollar you have

is the dollar
you lend me
for your sake."
Christ says:
"You cannot
serve two masters,
God and Mammon."
"You cannot,
and all our education
is to try to find out
how we can
serve two masters,
God and Mammon,"
says Robert Louis Stevenson.